AN ILLUSTRATED H

Dreadnoughts

AN ILLUSTRATED HISTORY

Dreadnoughts

GERALD TOGHILL

AMBERLEY

First published 2019

Amberley Publishing
The Hill, Stroud
Gloucestershire, GL5 4EP

www.amberley-books.com

British Library Cataloguing in Publication Data.
A catalogue record for this book is available from the British Library.

ISBN 978 1 4456 8635 6 (print)
ISBN 978 1 4456 8636 3 (ebook)

Origination by Amberley Publishing.
Printed in Great Britain.

Contents

Introduction

The twentieth century was witness to an unprecedented expansion in the shipbuilding industry, so much so that preceding generations could not possibly have envisaged it. The Industrial Revolution together with the increasing ease with which metal could be

HMS *Warrior*, *c.* 1860. The direct ancestor of all dreadnoughts; her appearance on the naval scene in 1860 revolutionised the world's navies.

worked, burgeoning technology and manufacturing businesses springing up all over meant that, for shipbuilders, the world became their oyster. With arms races developing around the world and two world wars in the first half of the century, it is small wonder that shipbuilding sales went through the roof as more and more ships were required, both commercial and military.

Not least among the shipbuilders' customers was the British Admiralty due to their policy of maintaining a navy at least equal to any two navies that might be considered potential adversaries. This was an expensive policy, but it meant that there was nowhere in the world where a Royal Navy ship could not suddenly appear over the horizon and her merchant fleet, safe in that knowledge, confidently swelled accordingly. Britain became the world leader in ship design and building, and all over the British Isles shipyards, big and small, flourished to the extent that at least half the world turned to Britain to build their commercial vessels and their warships.

In this atmosphere it was only a matter of time before someone – in this case the French – envisaged employing the now easily and reasonably cheaply obtained iron to protect their warships. With this development linked to steam-powered machinery, the naval scene was ripe for an explosion of innovation.

Before the Dreadnought

Naval construction before the dreadnoughts had been particularly active, spurred on by the French Navy launching their imaginative 5,529-ton *Gloire* in November 1859.

This was the world's first ocean-going ironclad; indeed, she was a true ironclad because her 30-inch-thick wooden hull was covered with 4.7-inch-thick wrought-iron plates. Bristling with guns, some of which were rifled, firing explosive shells that had unheard of destructive power against wooden ships, she frightened the British Admiralty half to death, and when it was announced that she would have two sister ships, the Admiralty could see their carefully crafted policy of superiority over two or more of their rivals rapidly disappearing.

The response was utterly astonishing, driven by a determination to build a ship so superior that it would be out of the question for France or any other nation to take Britain on in a sea battle. Before long, this was achieved.

At 9,210 tons, *Warrior* was nearly twice the size of *Gloire*, but the truly revolutionary thing about her was that she was the first iron-built ship. A wooden hull covered by iron plates was not for her; *Warrior* was all iron, from her keel all the way up through her frames and knees. When, at the cost of £377,292, she was completed and commissioned in August 1861, she was the largest, fastest and most powerfully armed warship in the world. Like *Dreadnought* some forty or so years later, her appearance rendered every warship in the world obsolete. Emperor Napoleon III of France summed her up by saying she was 'like a black snake among rabbits'.

There now opened up a whole new concept in naval warship building when construction, guns, engines, armour, all aspects of the art were led by the nose by technology. The huge advances in manufacturing evolving from the Industrial Revolution allowed for bigger, better guns, stronger, heavier armour, and faster, more powerful steam engines.

Throughout the latter half of the nineteenth century, maritime nations churned out bigger, better, stronger battleships, mounting heavier armour and ever bigger guns capable of firing over longer and longer distances, and led by Britain they churned out class after class of ponderous Leviathans, each improving in one way or another on its predecessor. It was, however, the increased ranges of the guns that really brought about the dreadnoughts.

One of the most important operations to be carried out when the guns spoke was the observation of the fall of shot, as the gunners needed to know where their shots were falling, but as ranges increased this became more and more difficult. During this period the evolution of the battleship from *Warrior* onwards had followed along the lines of a mixed armament – typically four 12-inch guns supported by ten or so of 9.2-inch calibre, which, in turn, were supported by a varying number of 6-inch ones. But this mixture now created problems in 'spotting' the fall of shot. At the increasing distances, and with all guns firing, it was almost impossible to differentiate between the splashes of the 12-, 9.2- or 6-inch shells. The gunnery worlds of all navies were clamouring for a solution until, necessity being the mother of invention, barely before the new twentieth century had cast off its baby clothes, a solution came to light.

HMS Swiftsure, c. 1903. One of the last of the Royal Navy's pre-dreadnoughts, she served during the war in the Mediterranean, returning to the UK in 1916 to be reduced to the Reserve as an accommodation ship. Post-war she was used as a target until going to the breakers in 1920. (Luis Photos, Gibraltar)

The Birth of *Dreadnought*

HMS *Dreadnought* – the ship that shook the world. (Luis Photos, Gibraltar)

The commonly held belief that the creation of the revolutionary battleship *Dreadnought*, launched in 1906, was purely the brainchild of the First Sea Lord, Admiral Lord Fisher, is true up to a point because he was the catalyst. In reality, rather than a flash of inspiration on his part, she was a logical step in the design of British battleships.

At the turn of the century the eminent warship designers Deadman and Narbeth, who had worked on the recently built British battleships of the King Edward VII Class, had, at that time, been pressing for a heavier armament and gone so far as to propose an all-12-inch armament for future builds.

At the same time an Italian naval constructor, Vittorio Caniberti, had written an article for the 1903 edition of *Jane's Fighting Ships* further prosecuting the cause of an all-big-gun armament and, on his part, this was not merely speculation but was reinforced by perfectly feasible facts and figures.

Admiral Fisher, at that time the commander-in-chief of the Mediterranean Fleet, was not slow in taking on board Deadman and Narbeth's ideas and was sufficiently impressed by Caniberti to form a small committee with a view of investigating and planning along these lines. When he was relieved as C-in-C of the Mediterranean Fleet in 1904, he went to the Admiralty as the First Sea Lord and it was in this illustrious position, being a man of considerable persuasive powers and great influence, that he was able to confront the Board of Admiralty with his ideas, reminding them sharply of their position as the world's leaders in ship design. To bring home his argument, he provided over a score of designs that his committee had drawn up.

To boost Fisher's persuasive powers, intelligence was received at the Admiralty that the United States of America was getting a step ahead by designing and laying down the South Carolina Class of battleships, which would mount eight 12-inch guns with only a 3-inch armament in support.

Finally, in January 1905 the Admiralty's Committee on Design, besieged by pressures on all sides, met to consider the proposals and, remarkably for a committee, in just seven weeks came up with their final report. In doing so, they created a design that was to revolutionise battleship building throughout the world. So innovative was their brainchild, which was to be called *Dreadnought*, that the name became generic, with all subsequent battleships and battlecruisers being referred to as dreadnoughts, while all those built before her appearance fell into the category of pre-dreadnoughts.

From the moment she took shape, *Dreadnought* created an almost mesmeric list of records. This great ship of just under 18,000 tons, more than 2,000 tons bigger than contemporary battleships, was laid down, launched and completed all within a year and a day – a truly magnificent feat. Mounting ten 12-inch 45-calibre guns she had, in support, twenty-seven 12-cwt guns forming the secondary armament, but it was her engines that caused a sharp intake of breath in naval circles and created a certain amount of awe. For the very first time, a ship of this size was driven by turbines.

Turbine machinery had been already involved in successful experiments but always in much smaller vessels, never in a ship of this size. However, turbines had

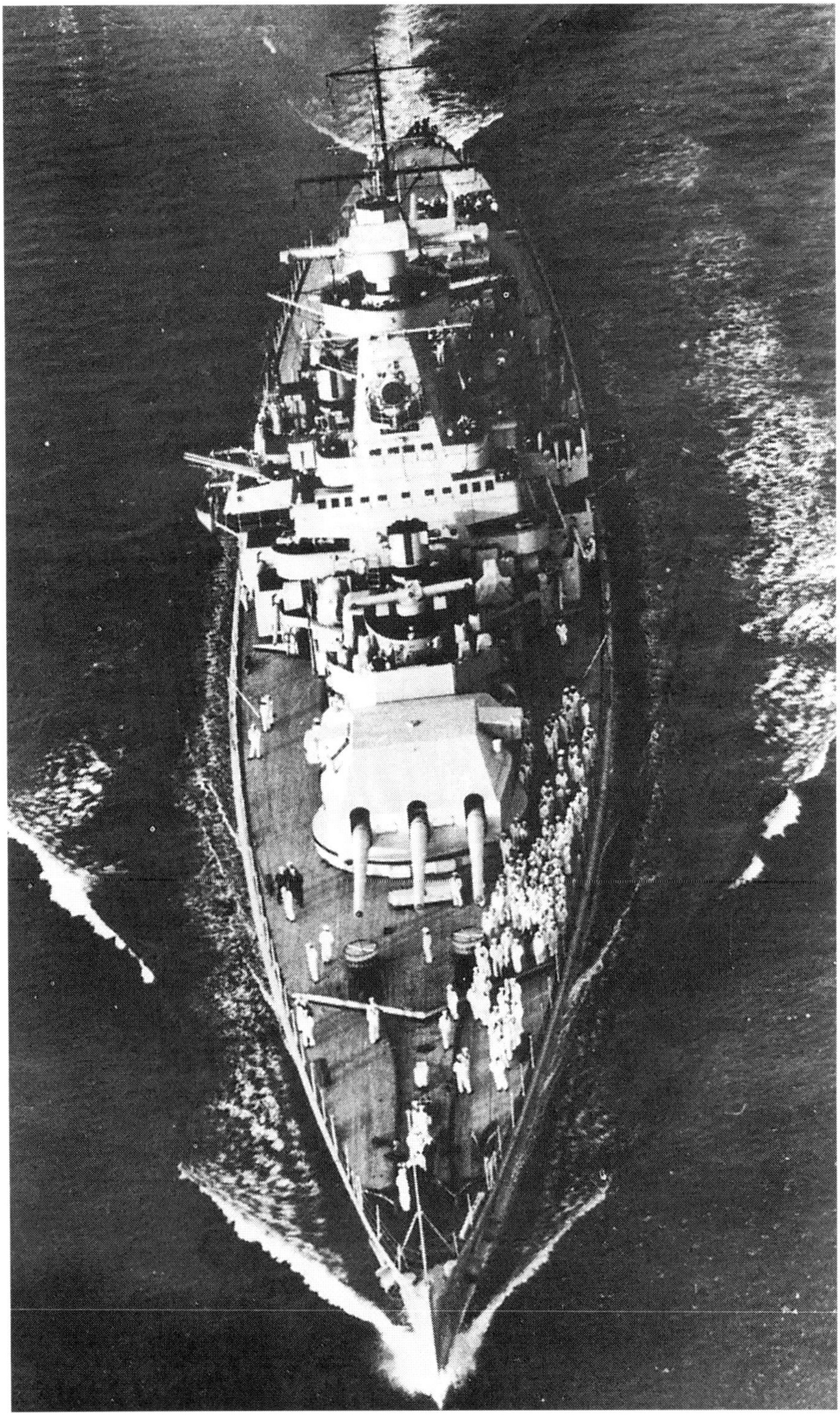

On the wrong end of a battleship's guns! (Author's collection)

a string of advantages: they created less vibration, were far more reliable at high speeds and allowed huge weight-saving. There were also fewer working parts in their make-up, making them easier to maintain, and this in turn meant fewer men were required to operate it. Additionally, because they were situated lower in the hull, they enjoyed increased protection. Finally, there would be a reduction in coal consumption at high speeds while producing an increase of some 5,000 shp. So, in line with being a true record breaker, she was the world's first major warship to be driven by turbines.

By the time she had completed her trials, the results of which were carefully leaked to the press, it was quickly realised throughout the world that in the whole of the existing huge battle fleets there was not a single warship that could face *Dreadnought* on anything like equal terms.

In 1912 there appeared a new name when the press coined the term 'super dreadnought' to describe Britain's new 25,870-ton Orion Class battleships, which had ten 13.5-inch guns mounted on the centre line in five twin turrets. This was considered to be an immense improvement on the previous dreadnoughts.

Great Britain Leads the Way

As mentioned, the British Admiralty at this time had a policy of maintaining a Royal Navy equal to any two of their contemporaries. In producing the magnificent *Dreadnought* they had almost bitten off more than they could chew, for such was her impact in the first years of the twentieth century leading up to the First World War that the whole international naval world was gripped by 'Dreadnought Fever'. A dreadnought became the number one on every maritime nation's 'must have' list as this mighty ship had rendered every other battleship in the world obsolete. Every nation capable of building such vessels was stung into a frenzy of building, while those maritime nations without the technology or capability of building them became eager customers for those who could. With the leading shipbuilders of the age being British, her shipyards there were laying down dreadnoughts as fast as they could for half the world's navies.

The Admiralty, in the meantime, had its own worries. There was the 'two-navy' superiority to maintain, so an immense building programme had to be authorised by Parliament. In private yards as well as the Royal Dockyards, vast supplies of steel were garnered from the steel mills, and mountains of metal began cluttering the yards.

At the same time the matter of ordnance was vigorously investigated. The manufacture of big guns was a very expensive and time-consuming process and, as with modern car manufacture, to build one car is not enough – many others have to be built in component parts to maintain the original one in working order, and so it was with the big guns. One outfit for each ship was not nearly enough as the wear and tear on the barrels was such that replacements were regularly being called for, so gun manufacture was of the utmost importance.

In December 1906, the Royal Dockyard at Portsmouth laid down the *Bellerophon*, the name ship of the 22,102-ton Class, just a month after *Dreadnought* had been launched. This was the first class of true 'dreadnoughts' and was the class that sent the world scrambling to join in what was termed 'Dreadnought Fever'. They were virtually repeats of *Dreadnought,* but with a few refinements. Comprising *Bellerophon*, *Superb*, built on the Tyne at Elswick, and *Temeraire*, built at Devonport Dockyard, they were all launched in 1907 and were completed in 1909. They led a sedate life, seeing the greater part of their service in the Home Fleet and, when it was formed in 1914, the Grand Fleet. Being the forerunners of the type, they were fairly outdated by the time the First World War burst upon the scene, but nonetheless they fulfilled a role in the Grand Fleet's battle squadrons and at the Battle of Jutland in 1916 formed the 4th Division of the 4th Battle Squadron under the command of Vice Admiral Sir Doveton Sturdee – a battle from which all three vessels emerged unscathed before then settling down to a routine of patrols in the North Sea.

Post-war, *Bellerophon* was considered so obsolete that she spent the rest of her days as a gunnery drill ship until sold out of service in 1921. *Superb* was deployed to the Mediterranean after the war and as fleet flagship led the fleet through the Dardanelles after the surrender of Turkey. She, too, was reduced to the role of gunnery drill ship in 1919, until being sold to a ship-breaker in 1921. The last of the class, *Temeraire*, also deployed to the Mediterranean after the war, assumed the role of training ship for cadets until being sold a year after her sisters.

Almost without drawing breath after the launch of *Temeraire*, Devonport laid down the *Collingwood* in 1907, one of the three 23,030-ton St Vincent Class, with the other two, *St Vincent*, being laid down at Portsmouth in 1907, and *Vanguard*, being laid down the following year at Barrow-in-Furness. Following mainly along the lines of the

HMS *Bellerophon* was laid down at Portsmouth Royal Dockyard just one month after *Dreadnought* had been launched. Note the web of wireless aerials. (Luis Photos, Gibraltar)

preceding class, they had one or two modifications, the main one being in armament. Abandoning the tried and trusted 45-calibre Mark X 12-inch gun, the St Vincents mounted ten of the 50-calibre Mark XI 12-inch guns (5 x 2) but they were not a success. Their high muzzle velocity caused excessive wear on the barrels, shortening their life, and at long range they were considerably less accurate. Added to this was the problem of smoke interference experienced in the after fire-control position, which made it all but inoperable.

All their service was in home waters, firstly with the Home Fleet and then, when it was formed in 1914, the Grand Fleet. At the Battle of Jutland *Vanguard* was with *Bellerophon* in the 4th Division of the 4th Battle Squadron, while the other two formed the 5th Division with the battleship *Neptune*. All three of the class emerged from the battle unscathed, but in 1917 *Vanguard* suffered a catastrophic accident. While at anchor at Scapa Flow, at 23.20 on 9 July she was suddenly ripped apart by an internal explosion. A subsequent enquiry concluded that the explosion was probably caused by a shell or charge igniting in a magazine. She sank very quickly – almost instantly – and with only two survivors, there were 804 lives lost. The loss of life in the explosion is still the most catastrophic accidental loss of life through explosion in the history of the UK and one of the worst accidental losses in the history of the Royal Navy. Not surprisingly, the site of her wreck is designated as a controlled site under the Protection of Military Remains Act and the subsequent court of inquiry following her destruction concluded that the explosion might have been caused by defective cordite, resulting in all the cordite in the fleet being changed and more vigorous magazine rounds instituted.

The remaining two vessels of the class survived the war, with *St Vincent* paying off at the end of the war and being reduced to the Reserve, where she remained until being sold in 1921. The last of the class, *Collingwood*, also reduced to the Reserve in 1919, acted as a gunnery training ship until being sold in 1922. Her main claim to fame was that at the Battle of Jutland one of her turret officers, a lieutenant, was the future King George VI.

The 19,900-ton single ship *Neptune*, built at Portsmouth Dockyard, was launched in 1909 and incorporated a number of 'firsts'. She was the first to have her midships turrets staggered so that breaks in the superstructure allowed them to fire across the ship, thus increasing the weight of her broadsides as all ten of her 12-inch guns would bear on either beam. Another 'first' was the addition of cruising turbines, which came into operation when steaming at moderate speeds and this reduced fuel consumption. One more 'first' concerned her after turrets, which, for the first time in a Royal Navy battleship, were superimposed. This was a system that, in this case, allowed less increase in length, which would have been required for the staggering of the midships turrets. Initially with the Home Fleet and then the Grand Fleet during the war, she emerged unscathed from the Battle of Jutland and was reduced to the Reserve in 1919 prior to being sold in 1922.

The 23,050-ton Colossus Class, comprising *Colossus* and *Hercules*, were laid down in 1909, launched in 1910 and completed in 1911.

HMS *Colossus*. As flagship of the 5th Division at the Battle of Jutland she received two hits and suffered five casualties. (Luis Photos, Gibraltar)

Both were products of commercial yards – Scotts and Palmers respectively – and both joined the Home Fleet when commissioned. In the Grand Fleet they took part in the Battle of Jutland, with *Colossus* as flagship of the 5th Division of the 1st Battle Squadron, where she had the misfortune to be hit in the battle. In fact she was hit twice, one of which was a shell that burst on the port side abaft the funnel, resulting in five casualties. Post-war, *Colossus* was reduced to a training role for cadets at Devonport until she was stricken in 1921, although she remained as a hulk at Devonport until finally being sold in 1928 to be broken up. Her sister ship went on to finer things; in November 1918 she conveyed the Armistice Commission to Kiel, assuming the role of flagship of the Commission there, but once back in the UK she was reduced to the Reserve and was sold to be broken up in 1921.

The Colossus Class was followed by the 25,850-ton Orion Class, comprising *Conqueror*, *Monarch*, *Orion* and *Thunderer*, which were launched in 1909/10. *Orion*, as lead ship, was laid down at Portsmouth Dockyard in June 1909, but the other three had to wait until April the following year before their keels took shape in commercial yards. Careful investigation into the matter of barrel wear in the big guns had ascertained that wear effect was linked to muzzle velocity and that wear in a barrel increased with greater velocity. It had also been proven that the hitting power of larger guns could be increased with reduced muzzle velocity, so the Orions mounted ten 13.5-inch 45-calibre Mark V guns on the centre line with superimposed turrets both forward and aft – the first ships so built. With their super-firing turrets, and being somewhat larger than their predecessors, they quickly earned the name 'super dreadnoughts'. Their service was entirely in home waters, firstly in the Home Fleet and then the Grand Fleet, forming the 2nd Division of the 2nd Battle Squadron. In this role they took part in the Battle of Jutland in 1916, from which they emerged totally unscathed. Post-battle their lives settled down into an unexciting routine of training and North Sea patrols. By the war's end in 1918 such had been the advances in battleship design they were considered obsolete, so they were paid off and reduced to the Reserve. Their end, though dragging on for a while, was always in sight and in 1922 both *Orion* and *Conquerer* wended their way to the breakers' yards, while the other two laboured on for a little while longer. *Monarch*, having been hulked as a stationary training ship at Devonport, was used as a target early in 1925. All sorts of abuse was hurled at her – bombing by aircraft and gunnery from battleships and cruisers – but through it all she stubbornly refused to succumb until the battleship *Revenge* blasted her at close range and she sank beneath the waves. *Thunderer* was the last survivor of the class and, having fulfilled a training role post-war, was towed away to the breakers in 1926. She, too, had a stubborn streak and while in tow she broke away and took the ground. Concerted efforts finally broke her free and she made the acquaintance of the searing torches in the breakers' yard.

With the launch of the Orions, the British yards now had the bit firmly between their teeth and 1911/12 hailed the 25,700-ton King George V Class, comprising *King George V*, *Centurion*, *Audacious* and *Ajax*. Although their lines were somewhat angular, they were considered to be the most handsome ships. There would be no battleships to match their beauty for over thirty years until the arrival of *Vanguard*.

On the debit side their secondary armament came in for a lot of criticism, limited as it was to sixteen 4-inch 50-calibre BL Mark VII; however, torpedo ranges had increased considerably, which meant that attacking destroyers and torpedo boats could fire from a greater distance, and it was felt that the 4-inch guns were not up to the mark in defending against such attacks. What would have been much more desirable would have been the current 6-inch guns, but the expense involved was not to the taste of the reigning Liberal government and so they remained under-gunned throughout their careers.

All four ships were laid down in 1911, with the lead ship entering the water at Portsmouth Dockyard in October of the same year. Portsmouth seemed to have the knack of speedy building – look at the *Dreadnought* being built and launched in a year and a day, for instance. *King George V* took somewhat longer, having been laid down on 16 January 1911 and completed in December 1912. *Centurion* was launched at Devonport Dockyard in late 1911, being completed in May 1913, and the last two, built in commercial yards, were completed in 1913. On commissioning they joined the Home Fleet and in 1914 helped form the newly inaugurated Grand Fleet.

Audacious had barely time to join the Grand Fleet when she had the misfortune to run afoul of a mine off Lough Swilly, Ireland, on 27 October 1914. Damage control – the containment of damage to a ship's hull – was an inexact science at that time and attempts to save her failed, especially after an internal explosion sometime after the mine increased damage. All attempts at towing failed in heavy weather and, well down

HMS King George V. With tall flat-sided funnels, she and her sister ships were thought of as very handsome, despite being under-gunned. (Luis Photos, Gibraltar)

by the stern, her crew were taken off without casualty by the armed merchant cruiser *Olympic*. Bizarrely, the only casualty throughout the whole incident was when she exploded, with a petty officer in the accompanying cruiser *Liverpool* some four cables distant being killed by flying debris.

When they were joined by the battleship *Erin*, the remaining three ships formed the 1st Division of the 2nd Battle Squadron in the Grand Fleet, with *King George V* assuming the role of flagship to Vice Admiral Sir Martyn Jerram, who was commanding the division. In this formation, they took part in the Battle of Jutland. After the battle their lives followed the humdrum routine of battleships in the Grand Fleet. Ever hopeful that the German High Seas Fleet would put to sea again, they carried out the dreary round of North Sea patrols and training duties. Post-war they were reduced to the Reserve in 1919, but were brought forward the following year to join the Mediterranean Fleet. *King George V* was the first to return from the Mediterranean in 1923 and took up a training role. The others followed her home in 1924 to be reduced to the Reserve.

The Washington Treaty now came into play, with the result being that *King George V* and *Ajax* were sold in 1926 to be broken up. *Centurion*, however, went on to lead a very interesting, not to say exciting, life. Having idled her life away in the Reserve from 1924, she was brought forward in 1926 and fitted out as a radio-controlled target ship for use in gunnery practices. This was to be her lot until, with another war raging in 1941, she was taken in hand for metamorphosing into a brand-new modern battleship.

In other words she was, with the addition of much timber and paint, made to look like the new battleship *Anson*, which was still being built. In her proud new livery she sailed all the way to Bombay via the Cape. Perhaps it was she who gave rise to the wonderful tale of being in company with other ships in rough weather when her forward turret was dislodged and washed overboard. To the utter astonishment of the people in the other ships, her great 13.5-inch turret, supposedly weighing over a hundred tons, complete with three 50-foot 'steel' barrels, bobbed along on the waves.

From Bombay she passed up through the Suez Canal to Alexandria, where she once more became a fighting ship of sorts. Mounting a number of 20-mm Oerlikon guns, she became an anti-aircraft ship at the mouth of the canal. She had a vital role to fulfil once more, which came about in 1944. Brought back to the UK, she was prepared as a blockship and went to war for the last time, crossing the Channel to Normandy, where she was sunk as part of the Mulberry Harbour.

While the King George V Class were still in the completion stage, the next set of keels was being laid. The Iron Duke Class was on its way. The lead ship was laid down in Portsmouth Dockyard in January 1912 and less than two weeks later at Devonport, great lines of steel representing the keel of the *Marlborough* appeared. At the end of

HMS *Iron Duke*. A casualty of the Washington Treaty, she still rendered service as a depot ship in the Second World War even after she had been sunk by air attack and settled to the bottom of Scapa Flow. (Luis Photos, Gibraltar)

May at Beardmore's yard on the Clyde the keel of *Benbow* was laid and just one day later many miles to the south the keel of the last of the class, *Emperor of India*, was laid down by Vickers at Barrow-in-Furness. The two in the Royal Dockyards were completed before the outbreak of war, but those in the commercial yards were not ready for sea until the First World War had commenced. Only a few months later all four vessels had joined the Grand Fleet, where they were involved in all the fleet's main excursions, including the Battle of Jutland, although at that event *Emperor of India* was absent, being docked down. The other three were not only in the battle but were all flagships: *Benbow* was a unit of the 4th Division of the 4th Battle Squadron and flagship of the division commander, Vice Admiral Sir Doveton Sturdee; while *Marlborough* was in the 6th Division of the 1st Battle Squadron as flagship of Vice Admiral Sir Cecil Burney. But it was *Iron Duke* that had the plum job; in the 3rd Division of the 4th Battle Squadron, she was not only flagship of the division, but flagship of the commander-in-chief of the Grand Fleet, Admiral Sir John Jellicoe.

Post-war, *Iron Duke* was deployed to the Mediterranean Fleet, which she joined in 1919 and where, for the next seven years, she basked in the warm Mediterranean sunshine. During the Russian Civil War she sailed through the Bosphorus to carry out operations against the Bolsheviks in the Black Sea, but in 1926 she moved out of the Mediterranean into the less hospitable waters of the Atlantic to join the Atlantic Fleet, in which she was to serve until 1929, when she was reduced to a training ship. At this stage a section of her armament was unshipped and she remained in this role until the outbreak of the Second World War, which saw her deployed to Scapa Flow for employment in the defence of the anchorage. At the same time, she became a depot ship. In October, no sooner had she had taken up her position in the Flow, than she was subjected to a heavy attack by German bombers and sustained considerable damage. To save her from sinking she was run aground, and so she remained with her bottom resting comfortably on the seabed, continuing to serve in her role as a depot ship and gun platform throughout the war. At the end of the conflict she was refloated and taken away to the breakers' yard in 1946, the last of a very noble class.

Her sister ships shadowed *Iron Duke* for most of their careers – serving with the Grand Fleet during the war, soaking up the balmy airs of the Mediterranean from 1919 to 1926, serving with the Atlantic Fleet until 1929 and then going for disposal. *Benbow* was the first to go, being sold out of the service to break up early in 1931, but *Marlborough* was to survive for over a year longer, being dragged off to the breakers in June 1932. *Emperor of India*, meanwhile, was still offering her services as a target until, having sustained untold punishment from the fleet's guns, she finally sank in September 1931.

The year 1913 saw the launch of two of the Royal Navy's most famous battleships. The 31,500-ton ships of the Queen Elizabeth Class, *Queen Elizabeth* and *Warspite*, roared down the slipways in the Royal Dockyards at Portsmouth and Devonport respectively, and in the same year the keels of the other three ships in the class were laid down in commercial yards.

Valiant, built on the Clyde by Fairfield, and *Barham*, also built on the Clyde but by John Brown, would be launched in September and October of 1914 respectively,

HMS *Queen Elizabeth* was lead ship and class name of four ships that served valiantly through two world wars. All bar one, *Barham*, survived both conflicts only to be broken up in the 1950s. (Luis Photos, Gibraltar)

followed by their sister ship *Malaya* from Armstrong's yard on the Tyne the year after. *Malaya* is worthy of a mention in her own right. The 1912 programme allowed for the building of a battlecruiser, but at the same time the Federated Malay States came up with the offer of paying for the building of a battleship, an offer that was gratefully accepted by the British Admiralty, and the building of the battlecruiser was put on hold. In appreciation of their generosity, the fifth ship of the class was named *Malaya*.

When commissioned, *Malaya* followed her sisters into the Grand Fleet joining the 5th Battle Squadron, in which role she took part in the Battle of Jutland in 1916. She sustained eight large shell hits during the battle, one of which struck a 6-inch battery, setting the ready-use ammunition alight. The fire resulted in 100 casualties, sixty-three of whom subsequently died. *Malaya* served through the Second World War, being finally broken up in 1948.

There was to have been a sixth ship in the class, *Agincourt*, but as she had not been laid down by the commencement of the First World War she was cancelled. It was at

HMS *Malaya* – a very generous gift from the Federated Malay States. (Author's collection)

this time that there was talk of a fast division in the fleet, and in furtherance of this, in 1913 there had been a move to build three Queen Elizabeth Class battleships at the expense of Canada, but the Canadian Naval Aid Bill, as it was termed, failed to make its way through the Canadian Parliament thanks to fierce filibustering by the Liberal opposition. The bill failed and this put paid to the idea of an eight-ship fast wing.

The class saw much action during the First World War. With the exception of *Queen Elizabeth*, they took part in the Battle of Jutland in 1916 as units of the 5th Battle Squadron, with *Barham* leading as flagship of RA Evan-Thomas. Subsequent to the battle *Queen Elizabeth* became the flagship of Admiral Jellicoe, the commander-in-chief of the Grand Fleet, and it was onboard her that the German surrender was signed in November 1918.

Post-war there was very little rest for her. When the Grand Fleet was disbanded in 1918, she moved directly to the Atlantic Fleet, in which she served until going to the Mediterranean in 1924. She remained in the Mediterranean continuously until returning to the UK in 1937, although she had some sort of break when she was taken in hand for refitting in 1926–27. On her return to the UK she was paid off to be taken in hand for an extensive reconstruction. By the time she completed her rebuild in January 1941 the fury of another European war was once more raging and she immediately returned to the Mediterranean, where she had her share of excitement. In December of that year she was subjected to an attack by Italian 'human torpedoes' while in the supposed security of Alexandria Harbour. Suffering considerable damage, she was patched up in situ sufficient for her to steam to Norfolk, Virginia, for permanent repair, which took until June 1943. Back in the UK she worked up and then deployed to the Eastern Fleet at Trincomalee in December.

Assuming the role of flagship of the Eastern Fleet, she was very busy along the coasts of Burma and Malaya until returning to the UK in July 1945. Exhausted, she crept away into the Reserve Fleet allowing her 'clapped out' engines to shudder to a permanent stop. In utter peace and quiet she remained dormant in the Portsmouth Reserve until sold for breaking in 1948. In tow she slowly wended her way up the west coast of the UK to the Clyde, where she was greeted by Arnott Young at Dalmuir, Clydebank, to be broken up.

Warspite was probably the most famous warship in the Royal Navy's history and throughout her lifetime was seldom out of the news, especially as she had a formidable record for sustaining damage in both war and peace. Twice in 1915, the first year of her life, she came to grief, firstly when she ripped out her bottom by running over the Dumbarton Reef in the Firth of Forth at 14 knots, requiring her to be docked down for bottom repairs. Then, no sooner had she rejoined the fleet after being repaired than she collided with her sister ship *Barham* and went back to the dockyard for more repairs. At the Battle of Jutland in 1916 she was in the 5th Battle Squadron and inflicted much damage on a number of German ships with her first-class shooting until her helm jammed and she went into high-speed circles, which took her into near point-blank range of German guns. She received thirteen heavy shell hits, miraculously managing to escape with very few casualties, but was forced to retire. As she limped towards Rosyth Dockyard she was attacked by a German submarine, which fired two torpedoes at her. Fortunately for her, both missed by a hair's breadth. Taken in hand at Rosyth on 1 June for repairs, she was completed on 22 July and rejoined the fleet.

More battle damage and another collision followed in 1917, a grounding in 1928 and another collision in 1933. She was damaged in action in 1941, 1943 and 1944, and was finally grounded on her way to the breakers' yard. Of all these mishaps, only four were in action.

She had a 'gremlin' that thrived down in her bowels, residing in her steering gear. Several times in her career the 'gremlin' struck and each time her steering jammed sending her around in circles as it had at Jutland in 1916. Post-war she followed the usual round experienced by most battleships in a peacetime role: Atlantic Fleet, refit, Mediterranean Fleet, back to the Atlantic Fleet and when that fleet was disbanded, the Home Fleet. In 1934 she was taken in hand for a three-year major reconstruction, emerging from that in 1937 virtually a new ship, and went back to the Mediterranean.

Her Second World War career took off when she returned to the UK in 1940 to take a leading part in the Norwegian Campaign, after which it was back to the Mediterranean as flagship. Involved in almost continuous action, she sustained bomb damage during the Crete operations and retired to Alexandria for temporary repairs. Fit for sea she transited the Suez Canal to Singapore on her way to Seattle, USA, for permanent repairs. Fully repaired, she joined the Eastern Fleet in January 1942, but the following year her big guns were needed back in the Mediterranean to cover the

HMS *Warspite* was described by the commander-in-chief of the Mediterranean Fleet in the Second World War as being the 'Grand Old Lady', and 'when she lifts her skirts she can really move'. In all the major actions of two world wars she was awarded more battle honours than any other ship in the long history of the Royal Navy. (Luis Photos, Gibraltar)

HMS *Valiant* is shown employing her crane to hoist her seaplane inboard. It was the practice at this time for the aircraft to be catapulted into the air and to then land alongside the ship to be hoisted inboard by crane. (Luis Photos, Gibraltar)

Salerno Landings in September. Seldom out of trouble, she sustained yet more damage from two glider bombs, resulting in massive flooding in her boiler rooms. Limping off to Malta, she received 'first aid', and again at Gibraltar, until she arrived in the UK to be taken in hand at Rosyth for permanent repairs commencing in March 1944.

However, momentous events were to overtake her and once more her great guns were demanded to cover landings, this time the greatest landings of all time. Still not fully repaired, with the holes in her side filled with cement, she headed south to the Normandy beaches. Such was her rate of fire that by 11 June she desperately needed a change of gun barrels, so she sailed for Rosyth. Trouble struck again on passage when she was severely damaged by a mine off Harwich and crawled painfully into Rosyth. Partially patched up she steamed off again to the bombardment areas and was in action at Brest, Le Havre and Walcheren but these were her last actions. Exhausted, thoroughly clapped out, leaking like a sieve she lay abandoned in the Reserve at Portsmouth with her great guns stripped out until she was finally sold in 1946 to break up. But she was not done yet! In tow off the Cornish coast in heavy weather on 23 April 1947, game to the last, she broke free and headed for the shore, taking the ground at Prussia Cove near to St Michael's Mount. Stuck fast, she refused to move and had to be broken up in situ. The mighty *Warspite* was to collect a total of sixteen battle honours more than any other Royal Navy ship in history.

The Queen Elizabeth Class was to serve tenaciously throughout both world wars. The first two of this class were followed by numbers three and four in 1914, *Valiant* and *Barham*. Not only did they all survive the First World War, but with one exception they came through the Second World War too. The exception was *Barham*, which sank after a German submarine hit her with three torpedoes in the Mediterranean in November 1941. She had the dubious distinction of being the first battleship to be sunk in the open sea since the battleship *Britannia* in November 1918, almost exactly twenty-three years before.

With the prospect of a great European conflict looming ominously over the land, the British building yards went into overdrive. The last pre-war British class, the five ships of the 31,000-ton Royal Sovereign Class, were launched in 1913/14.

Ramillies, *Resolution*, *Revenge*, *Royal Oak* and *Royal Sovereign* all served in the battle squadrons of the Royal Navy's Grand Fleet during the conflict. They all survived to serve in the Second World War although *Royal Oak* saw little action being torpedoed in 1939 while in harbour just one month into the war. She sank with heavy loss of life and was subsequently declared a war grave.

Though the Royal Sovereigns was the last class to be built pre-war, there were three other battleships in the British fleet at the outbreak of the war, each with an unusual origin. Beginning life in Armstrong's yard at Elswick-on-Tyne, the *Rio De Janeiro* was being built for the Brazilian government. However, in the early part of 1914 the Brazilians decided that she was a little rich for their blood and in an uncompleted state she was put up for sale. Into the breach stepped the Turkish government, purchasing her for something over £2 million, and construction continued under the new name of *Sultan Osman I*. However, war broke out before she could be delivered to her new owners and the First Lord of the Admiralty, Winston Churchill, ordered that she be

HMS *Barham* seen in heavy weather in the South Atlantic *c*. 1930. (Evan Williams)

seized. Thus, as HMS *Agincourt* she was taken into the Royal Navy. She was, at this time, reputed to be the most powerful battleship in the world on account of her unusual armament, featuring no fewer than seven 12-inch twin turrets and twenty 6-inch guns.

In a similar vein, another Turkish battleship was under construction at Barrow-in-Furness – the 25,250-ton *Reshadieh*. Almost complete at the outbreak of the war, she was requisitioned into the Royal Navy under the name of *Erin*. Throughout the conflict she served in the British Grand Fleet, operating mainly in the North Sea until she was reduced to the Reserve in 1919. The following year she was discarded under the terms of the Washington Treaty. She remained in the Reserve for a while but her fate was sealed and in 1922 she was sold. The following year she was broken up at Queensferry.

Also being built at Armstrong's yard were two battleships for the Chilean Government, the 32,120-ton *Almirante Latorre* and the *Almirante Cochrane*. They were both requisitioned into the Royal Navy but only the first vessel was completed as a battleship, under the name of *Canada*. Her sister ship was converted into the 22,790-ton aircraft carrier *Eagle*.

A veteran of both world wars, HMS *Royal Sovereign* was transferred into the Russian Navy in 1944, returning to the Royal Navy in 1949 to be immediately sold to the breakers. (Author's collection)

With the severe restrictions imposed by the Great Depression upon all aspects of life during the 1930s, the Royal Navy engaged in no further dreadnought building until it was almost the very cusp of the Second World War. With the threat of war once again looming the Treasury relaxed its iron grip, allowing a class of battleships to be ordered in 1937. By this time all treaty restrictions had lapsed, so the five-ship King George V Class (the second British class of that name) weighed in at 40,076 tons. Comprising *King George V*, *Prince of Wales*, *Duke of York*, *Anson* and *Howe*, this was a class that was to achieve fame and provide sterling service in the forthcoming conflict.

Another class of battleships, the 46,000-ton three-ship Lion Class, was projected, of which two, *Lion* and *Temeraire*, were actually laid down in 1939, but the third, *Thunderer*, never even reached that stage. They were envisaged under the escalation clause of the London Treaty, which allowed for ships of 45,000 tons and an armament comprising 16-inch guns. Accordingly, this class was each to carry nine 16-inch guns, which fired 2,375-lb shells, mounted in triple turrets, but thereby lay the snag. The 16-inch guns entailed no mean feat of engineering in their manufacture. Each 16-inch gun was 50 calibre, that is to say the barrel from breech face to muzzle was fifty times

HMS *Resolution*. At the grand old age of thirty-five she met her end in the breakers' yard, in 1948. (Author's collection)

HMS *Ramillies* suffered an attack by a Japanese midget submarine at Diego Suarez in 1942. (Author's collection)

Unscathed at the Battle of Jutland in 1916, HMS *Revenge* served throughout the Second World War at home and in the Far East. (Luis Photos, Gibraltar)

the diameter of the bore: i.e. fifty times 16 inches, which equals a barrel length of 66.6 feet weighing in at a cool 119.5 tons.

Not surprisingly the manufacture of these huge guns, together with the turrets to hold them, proved to be a long and drawn-out process, which had a projected timescale of at least four years before the whole outfit of guns could be completed. This meant that they would not be ready for use until 1943, and that was always supposing that, in war-torn Britain with materials in short supply, there were no unexpected hold-ups. Work on the two ships that had been laid down was therefore abandoned and the whole project was dropped.

Ex-Turkish *Sultan Osman I* and ex-Brazilian *Rio De Janeiro*, HMS *Agincourt* was the most heavily armed battleship the Royal Navy ever operated. She was sold to the breakers in 1922 as another casualty of the Washington Treaty. (Luis Photos, Gibraltar)

Ex-Turkish *Reshadieh*, HMS *Erin* was seized by the British in 1914 while completing in the UK. (Luis Photos, Gibraltar)

Ex- Chilean *Almirante Latorre*, HMS *Canada's* outstanding feature was her enormous funnel. Having served in the British Battle Fleet throughout the First World War, she was re-purchased by Chile and resumed her original name. (Luis Photos, Gibraltar)

A dramatic artistic impression of the battleship *King George V.* (Author's collection)

HMS *King George V* from the first class of British dreadnoughts built post-treaty restrictions. (Author's collection)

A 16-inch gun barrel. (US Naval History & Heritage Command)

War-torn and weary! HMS *Resolution* and HMS *Valiant* are seen reduced to training ship mode as part of the 'Imperieuse' training organisation at Devonport in 1944. (Evan Williams)

British Battlecruisers

While *Dreadnought* was still being built, the indefatigable 'Jacky' Fisher unleashed onto an unsuspecting world another of his great innovations – the battlecruiser. Fisher incorrectly foresaw the Baltic as a prime operational area in any future conflict and wanted vessels that could cope with the shallower waters encountered there. At the same time he required these ships to be as heavily armed as any contemporary battleship but to be lighter and faster than existing, or even future, battleships. Thus the battlecruiser was born. This was still a dreadnought, but with refinements and one or two failings.

In comparison to contemporary battleships, they had all of Fisher's requirements. The early classes mounted eight 12-inch guns and were capable of 25 knots, but there would soon be refinements, with later ones achieving 28 knots and mounting eight 13.5-inch guns. Even this upgrade was not the end. In 1916 Britain's *Renown* and *Repulse* were commissioned, each mounting six massive 15-inch guns and which, despite their heavier guns, were capable of no less than 31.5 knots, far exceeding the speed of all contemporary battlecruisers. These assets exactly fulfilled Fisher's requirements – fast, powerful ships that could chase an enemy, assets that had been ably demonstrated at the Falklands and again at Heligoland.

However, with there being no such thing as a free lunch, these assets had to be paid for and the only currency available was armour. Whereas contemporary battleships would carry 12 inches or more of steel armour around their sides, the battlecruisers had to put up with just 6 inches in the scramble to save weight and there was little or no deck armour. A heavy price would be paid for this in the future.

This type of warship was not a great success worldwide due mainly to the cost involved. A lot of countries had very nearly bankrupted themselves in obtaining battleships to the extent that a trip down the battlecruiser road was much too rich for their blood. Accordingly, the only country to follow Britain's lead was Germany, and rather than an appreciation of the battlecruisers' worth, this was probably due to the Kaiser's blind enmity of the Royal Navy and his determination to try to keep pace with them, so that by 1914 there were seven such ships in the German Fleet.

The battlecruiser was most successful when employing its superior speed for running down slower, inferior ships, which their great guns could despatch quickly and efficiently. It was, however, not quite so clever when up against heavily armed ships, as was to be evidenced at the Battle of Jutland during the forthcoming conflict.

A conventional view of the battlecruiser HMS *Repulse*. (Author's collection)

The first of Fisher's brainchildren, the 17,255-ton *Indomitable*, leader of the three-ship Invincible Class, rolled noisily down Fairfield's slipway into the bitter waters of the Clyde on 16 March 1907.

The world's first battlecruiser was received with a certain amount of pride and considerable speculation in British naval circles. But the die was cast and battlecruisers were to become a significant arm of the Royal Navy, as was evinced shortly after when sister ship *Invincible* made the acquaintance of the Tyne from Armstrong's Elswick yard the following month. She was fated to meet her end tragically at the Battle of Jutland in 1916, when she was on the receiving end of just three salvos from German ships. One shell in the third salvo burst into 'Q' turret amidships, blowing off the roof and detonating the magazine. The unfortunate ship was blown in half and this probably detonated 'A' and 'X' magazines. In just ninety seconds she disappeared below the waves, taking all but six of her 1,026 men with her.

The last of the class, *Inflexible*, which had been built in John Brown's yard, was launched into the Clyde in June. She led a very active life, serving firstly in the Home Fleet and then in the Mediterranean as flagship of the C-in-C. Still in the

The world's first battlecruiser, HMS *Indomitable* was the fruition of Admiral 'Jacky' Fisher's plan to combine a battleship's armament on a shallower draught and an increased speed. (Luis Photos, Gibraltar)

Mediterranean at the outbreak of war as flagship of the 2nd Battlecruiser Squadron, during operations in the Dardanelles in 1915 she struck a mine, which killed thirty-two of her crew, forcing her to retire to Malta and then Gibraltar for repairs. Returning to the UK after repair she joined the Grand Fleet and with her sister ships formed the 3rd Battlecruiser Squadron – a role in which she took part in the Battle of Jutland in 1916. Post-war obsolescence overtook her and she kept an appointment with the breakers in 1921.

No sooner were the Invincibles in the water than the next class was being laid down. The 22,110-ton Indefatigable Class gave the Australians and New Zealanders a chance to have a battlecruiser of their very own. Australia kept hers as flagship of the Dominion's Navy, but New Zealand decided such a big ship was a bit rich for their purse and so gifted her to the Royal Navy. The leader of the class, *Indefatigable*, was built at Devonport Dockyard and launched in 1909. In the Grand Fleet's Battlecruiser Squadron she took part in the Battle of Jutland, but crossing swords with the German battlecruiser *Von Der Tann* she was hit several times and paid the penalty for reduced armour. It was deduced that one or more shells penetrated her magazines, which resulted in her blowing up in a most spectacular fashion. At full speed she rolled over and sank, taking with her all but three of her 850 people.

HMS *Invincible*, *c.* 1907. The second of the class, she failed to survive the First World War, being sunk at the Battle of Jutland on 31 May 1916, leaving just six survivors. (Luis Photos, Gibraltar)

The second in the class, *Australia*, was built by order of the Australian government and was constructed on the Clyde by John Brown. As soon as she was completed she headed south for Australia, where she became the Dominion's flagship. She started the war as flagship of a combined Anglo-Japanese squadron operating in the Pacific and South African waters, but in 1915 was deployed to the UK to join the Grand Fleet. Having been in a collision with sister ship *New Zealand*, she was docked down and missed being at the Battle of Jutland. The remainder of the war was spent as flagship of the 2nd Battlecruiser Squadron and post-war she returned to Australia to resume the role of flagship. A victim of the Washington Treaty, she was ceremoniously scuttled off Sydney in 1924.

The final ship of the class was *New Zealand*, built by order of the New Zealand government but gifted into the Royal Navy. Launched from Fairfield's Yard on the Clyde in 1911, she commissioned in 1913 and went off on a world cruise, visiting, among other places, New Zealand, and there she was presented with a 'magical' Maori skirt. It is reported that at the battles of Heligoland in 1914, Dogger Bank in 1915 and

Jutland in 1916, the captain wore the skirt over his uniform, and it was to this that their good fortune in the battles was attributed.

Post-war she was again sent off on a world cruise, this time carrying Admiral Jellicoe on a mission to examine the naval defences of the Dominions. In 1920 she was paid off for the last time, being reduced to the Reserve until, victim of the Washington Treaty, she was broken up in 1922.

Fisher's faith in battlecruisers continued. In 1912 the single 31,650-ton ship *Queen Mary* hit the water, followed in 1914 by another single ship, the 35,000-ton *Tiger* (*Lion* and *Tiger* soon became known as the 'Beautiful Cats').

At the commencement of hostilities in 1914, the Royal Navy boasted ten battlecruisers, plus one building, as well as twenty-five battleships with a further six building and nearing completion. This compared very favourably with Germany's eight battleships, with a further six building, and seven battlecruisers, with a further two building.

HMS *Inflexible*, *c*. 1907. The last of her class, she survived the hostilities of the First World War to be broken up in 1921. (Luis Photos, Gibraltar)

HMS *Indefatigable, c.* 1909. Lead ship of the class, fate overtook her at the Battle of Jutland in 1916 when she was hit by the German battlecruiser *Von Ver Tann*. At full speed she rolled over and sank, taking all but three of her 850 crew with her. (Luis Photos, Gibraltar)

HMAS *Australia*. Built by order of the Australian government, she served most of the First World War with the Grand Fleet. (Luis Photos, Gibraltar)

HMS *New Zealand*. Built by order of the New Zealand government, she was 'gifted' to the Royal Navy upon her completion. (Luis Photos, Gibraltar)

The two ships of the 31,310-ton Lion Class appeared on the scene at the turn of the first decade of the twentieth century. *Lion* was the first to be launched and she tasted the waters of the River Tamar at Devonport in August 1910. As flagship of the Battlecruiser Squadron throughout the First World War, she took part in all the major actions and accounted for a German cruiser during the Battle of Heligoland in 1914. At the Battle of Dogger Bank in 1915, however, she took sixteen hits from 11- or 12-inch German shells and was so badly damaged that she had to be towed back to Rosyth for urgent repair. Coming in for more punishment the following year at the Battle of Jutland, she suffered twelve hits from 12-inch shells, one of which was very nearly the end of her! A 12-inch shell smashed into the midship 'Q' turret, starting a serious fire. Had the fire been allowed to reach the magazine she would almost certainly have been destroyed, as had other battlecruisers, but the bravery of the turret officer, Major Harvey of the Royal Marine Light Infantry, saved the day. Already mortally wounded, he ordered the flooding of the magazine and so saved the ship – an action that was rewarded posthumously with the Victoria Cross. Post-war, *Lion* became another victim of the Washington Treaty and was sold to a breaker in 1924.

A picture postcard impression of the period showing HMS *New Zealand*. She served in the Grand Fleet throughout the First World War. (Evan Williams)

The other of the class, the *Princess Royal*, was launched from Vicker's Yard at Barrow-in-Furness in 1910 some eight months after her leader. Her first taste of action came at the Battle of Heligoland Bight in 1914, from which she emerged unscathed. Her luck held so that she came out of the following year's Battle of Dogger Bank also unscathed, but her luck deserted her at the Battle of Jutland where within minutes of the German ships opening fire she sustained hits. In all she suffered eight 12-inch hits and one 11-inch, suffering twelve killed and eighty-one wounded. Nevertheless, despite a number of fires burning and her mast damaged, she remained in the line. This was her last major action, although at the 2nd Battle of Heligoland Bight in 1917 she provided distant support. Post-war she too fell victim of the Washington Treaty and went off to the breakers in 1922.

In March 1912, Palmer's Yard at Jarrow-on-Tyne launched the 31,650-ton battlecruiser *Queen Mary*, which was to have a short but busy life. Sometimes referred to as the third ship in the Lion Class, she was really a single ship, and when completed in 1913 she joined the 1st Battlecruiser Squadron in the Home Fleet being with them when they visited Kronstadt, Russia, that year. After taking part in the royal review the following year, the squadron joined the newly formed Grand Fleet to prepare for war. She was at the Battle of Heligoland not long after war commenced, from which she emerged unscathed, but at the Battle of Jutland in 1916 her luck ran out. In the early stages of the battle she came up against the German battlecruiser *Derfflinger*'s 12-inch guns. A hit on 'Q' turret was followed by a straddle of 12-inch shells resulting

HMS *Lion*. Together with the battlecruiser *Tiger* they were known in naval circles as the 'Beautiful Cats'. (Luis Photos, Gibraltar)

in 'A' and 'B' magazines exploding, completely destroying the fore part of the ship. This was followed by another huge explosion – probably 'Q' magazine. In a massive fireball she disappeared, taking all her 1,266 men with her.

The second of the two ships to be known as the 'Beautiful Cats' was launched in 1913 by John Brown on the Clyde. The 55,710-ton single ship *Tiger*, the last Royal Navy dreadnought to burn coal, became a unit of the 1st Battlecruiser Squadron in the Grand Fleet in 1914 and had her first taste of battle at Dogger Bank in 1915 when she sustained six hits resulting in ten killed and eleven wounded. However, she lived to fight another day and at the Battle of Jutland the following year she expended over 300 rounds of 13.5-inch ammunition, claiming merely a miserable three hits on the enemy. In reply she was on the receiving end of fifteen hits, which resulted in twenty-four of her men being killed and forty-six wounded. Post-war she remained in service until the Washington Treaty caught up with her under the 'Age Clause' and she was earmarked for disposal, which came the following year when she was sold to be broken up.

The year 1916 saw the launch of a trio of ships that turned out to be neither fish, flesh nor fowl. Admiral Fisher wanted light, fast, but powerful ships that would be capable of taking part in amphibious operations on the German Baltic coast, and thus *Courageous*, *Glorious* and *Furious* were born. The first two were completed and

HMS *Princess Royal*'s luck ran out at the Battle of Jutland and she suffered nine big calibre hits killing twelve and wounding eighty-one of her crew. (Luis Photos, Gibraltar)

HMS *Queen Mary.* At the Battle of Jutland she and her 1,266 crew disappeared in a massive fireball. (Luis Photos, Gibraltar)

commissioned, but *Furious*, having been laid down, was converted into an aircraft carrier while still on the stocks.

With a displacement of less than 23,000 tons and much reduced armour protection, they were more like heavy cruisers than contemporary battlecruisers and most unsuitable for operations with the Grand Fleet, although this was where they fulfilled most of their service. Post-war, both ships were employed as gunnery training ships before being relegated to the Reserve. They were taken in hand in 1924 for conversion to aircraft carriers, in which guise they served in the Second World War.

In 1916 amid the furore of war the two battlecruisers of the 30,835-ton Renown Class were launched. *Repulse*, which had come to life in the yard of John Brown on the Clyde, was launched in August that year, followed quickly by *Renown* from Fairfield's yard also on the Clyde. Having survived hostilities they were saved from the Washington Treaty's deprivations and went on to serve in the next great conflict. However, in the 1930s they both underwent very serious rebuilds, with *Renown* being reconstructed to a far greater degree than her sister – so much so that when the Second World War broke out they were completely unrecognisable as sister ships. *Repulse* was to meet her end in 1941 when, in company with the battleship *Prince of Wales*, she was subjected to air attack by waves of Japanese aircraft. Hit by a number of aerial torpedoes, which caused extensive flooding, she settled in the water while most of her crew were taken off by accompanying destroyers. *Renown*, on the other hand, after

HMS *Tiger* – one of the 'Beautiful Cats'. Post-war she managed to elude the Washington Treaty until it caught up with her under the 'Age Clause' in 1931. (Luis Photos, Gibraltar)

Beneath the ungainly top hamper it is possible to just make out the battlecruiser hull of HMS *Furious*. (Author's collection)

Above and below: Together with their uncompleted sister ship *Furious,* HMS *Courageous* and *Glorious* were converted into aircraft carriers. (Luis Photos, Gibraltar)

spending an active war with the Home Fleet and in the Mediterranean, was reduced to a training ship post-war, until being sold off in 1948 to be broken up.

The last of the Royal Navy's battlecruisers was probably the most famous. The war years of 1916/17 had seen the laying down of another class of battlecruisers, the 45,200-ton Hood Class, which was to comprise *Hood*, *Rodney*, *Howe* and *Anson*. However, work progressed slowly and it wasn't until 1918 that the sole survivor of the class was launched when *Hood* left the slipway of John Brown's yard on the Clyde. Work on the other three had been intermittent, and they were cancelled in 1918.

HMS *Repulse* was as beautiful a ship as is ever likely to be seen. Her end came from waves of Japanese aircraft off the east coast of Malaya in 1941, with the loss of 513 men. (Luis Photos, Gibraltar)

HMS *Renown* served in both the Home Fleet and the Mediterranean in the Second World War. (Luis Photos, Gibraltar)

The 'Mighty *Hood*' was launched just three months before the Armistice in November 1918 so she saw no action in the First World War. It was not until 1920 that she joined the fleet as flagship of the Battlecruiser Squadron. In construction she was like no other battlecruiser due to the lessons learned regarding vulnerability to gunfire, and as a result her armour had been considerably increased. There was still a requirement for a fast ship, which could only be obtained by a long, lean hull, so with this, combined with her extra armour, she was longer and heavier than contemporary battleships.

Between the wars she garnered film star status and in company with the battlecruiser *Repulse* she was sent on a world cruise in 1923, taking in South Africa, Australasia and the United States. No matter where she went huge crowds flocked to the jetties to see her and her fame spread far and wide. She was the pride of the British Navy and the envy of every navy in the world. Ten months later she returned to the UK and took up residence in the Home and Atlantic fleets until she went to the Mediterranean in 1936. She remained in the sunshine until 1939, when she returned to the Home Fleet.

'The Mighty *Hood*' – wherever she went her 'film star' status drew huge crowds. (Luis Photos, Gibraltar)

Only eight minutes into the action, HMS *Hood* succumbed to *Bismark's* 15-inch guns, sinking with a massive explosion and leaving behind just three survivors. (Luis Photos, Gibraltar)

Heavy weather in the unforgiving Atlantic. (Evan Williams)

The complicated internal organs of a battlecruiser. (Author's collection)

She went to war with the Home Fleet but in June 1940 she joined Force H at Gibraltar and with them she took part in the controversial action with the French Fleet at Oran in July, returning to the Home Fleet just one month later.

She was in the fleet anchorage at Scapa Flow when intelligence was received that the German battleship *Bismark* had sailed. In company with the battleship *Prince of Wales* she sailed on 19 May to hunt for the German – a hunt that ended five days later when the German ships were sighted in the early hours of 24 May (Empire Day). She opened fire on the German battleship at a range of 25,000 yards (12.5 nautical miles), but only eight minutes into the action she was hit by plunging fire from *Bismark*'s 15-inch guns. She was ripped apart in a massive explosion thought to have been a magazine exploding and sank in just two minutes, leaving behind just three survivors. In the UK the navy and the public were stunned at the loss of this wonderful vessel.

Hood had been the last of the British battlecruisers to be built, but there had been plans in 1921 to build another class of very large ones. Bearing a drawing board name of 'G3 Type', they were to have been just under 54,000 tons displacement and were to mount nine 16-inch guns. It is hard to tell whether or not this was a serious venture but the mere threat to build them was a very potent bargaining tool at the Washington Treaty negotiations. Whichever it was, as soon as the treaty had been solemnised the class was cancelled, never having left the drawing board.

The First World War

Britain, having followed a policy of maintaining a navy at least as powerful as her two nearest rivals, was top of the power list at the outbreak of the First World War with twenty-two battleships and another thirteen being built, and ten battlecruisers, with another one building. To bolster these there were no fewer than forty pre-dreadnoughts at sea. This meant that Britain could field a very powerful battle fleet indeed and in her shipbuilding yards the cacophony of drills and riveters' hammers proceeded apace as more ships were prepared to slide into the water. In 1916 the hulls of the two 30,835-ton Renown Class battlecruisers were launched, *Renown* and *Repulse*, both of which had been built on the Clyde.

Thus was the stage set as the First World War commenced. There was still a mindset at the time that modern sea warfare would comprise mainly of long lines of dreadnoughts battering each other to death with their big guns. The course of the war would prove that this was as outdated as the army's high command insisting on sending cavalry to France!

The first two years of the conflict saw several fairly major battles, none of which provided a trial for dreadnoughts. The first of these, the Battle of Heligoland Bight, took place just three weeks into the war and involved light forces with the 1st Battlecruiser Squadron in support, and although the capital ships were in action at the end of the battle it wasn't really a test. Three months later, in November, the Battle of Coronel in South American waters was again no trial for dreadnoughts, and neither was the Battle of the Falklands the following month, although it did permit two of Britain's battlecruisers to test their mettle.

Just one month after that, in January 1915, the Battle of Dogger Bank involved a more serious engagement of both German and British battlecruisers. The outcome was a victory for the Royal Navy, even though a tactical error on the part of the British Admiral permitted the German squadron to escape. Nonetheless, in reply to the British losses of fifteen killed and eighty wounded, the German squadron sustained 945 men killed and many hundreds wounded – a definite victory for the Royal Navy's battlecruisers! However, the real outcome of this battle was not so much a victory as a learning curve. The German Navy was quick to take on board that it was imperative to prevent the flash from bursting shells reaching the

HMS *Repulse* – the ill-fated battlecruiser that succumbed to Japanese aircraft in 1941. (Author's collection)

magazines. Accordingly, German capital ships were modified to eliminate this danger. The British, on the other hand, failed to take on board this valuable lesson, with the result that some sixteen months later, at the Battle of Jutland, they were to lose five major capital ships in this way.

The first action to involve battleships occurred in the Dardanelles in 1915. If ever a naval campaign could be described as a shambles this was it, and the French and British Allies paid accordingly. Misdirection of sea power resulted in a conglomeration of battleships, battlecruisers and pre-dreadnoughts employed in bombarding roles in the confined waters of the Dardanelles Strait, where the Turkish forts proved far too strong for the assaults and resulted in a woeful loss of ships and men. By the time the Allies had withdrawn from the campaign they had lost five pre-dreadnoughts (four from Britain and one from France) and many hundreds of lives. Wisely, the British had seen fit to withdraw their dreadnoughts early on in the campaign, leaving the pre-dreadnoughts to bear the burden. At one stage in 1915 one of their newest, shiniest battleships, *Queen Elizabeth*, was employed bombarding the Turkish forts but, with the realisation of the danger involved, she was quickly withdrawn back to the UK and the Grand Fleet. The lesson was clear – capital ships were a liability when bombarding in restricted waters and this was a lesson Britain was to absorb.

Not until 1916 was there to be an opportunity for the Leviathans to form up into their pre-conceived battle squadrons and face each other. At long last, as May made way for a flaming June, the North Sea echoed to the thunder of great guns to an extent never before heard when the British and German battle fleets in their serried ranks met in the very first engagement of capital ships. What the protagonists could not have foreseen at that time was that not only was this the first blooding of the great battle fleets, it would also be their swansong. Never again would such huge battle fleets engage each other in the open sea. The Battle of Jutland is probably the most talked about, discussed, debated, written about and chewed over of any naval confrontation and the outcome is still debated over a hundred years later. Without doubt the British sustained the highest number of casualties, with five great ships being sent to the bottom of the sea, taking with them nearly 6,000 men. The Germans, on the other

Big ships require a big dry dock! This is the Gibraltar Dry Dock, which ensured that dreadnoughts of the Mediterranean Fleet could be docked down without having to return to the UK. (Luis Photos, Gibraltar)

hand, lost only one battleship and one battlecruiser, with some 3,000 casualties, but it was the German Navy which, when night fell, broke off the engagement and fled for home in an acknowledgement that they were never going to attain a victory over the British Fleet. With the exception of the occasional sortie by their battlecruisers, the German High Seas Fleet never again ventured into the North Sea until, at the end of the war, they left their harbours to surrender to the British Grand Fleet off the north of Scotland.

The First World War was the first conflict in the history of mankind where there had been weapons of war flying in the air – aircraft had arrived. The signing of the Armistice in November 1918 also heralded the death knell of the ponderous battle fleets; the following twenty years saw the development and rise of air power, for which the dreadnought was never going to be a match.

For the Royal Navy, with its worldwide commitments, there arose a problem that was in urgent need of a solution. If dreadnoughts were to be deployed to overseas stations then they would obviously require docking facilities either for routine maintenance or for repair. It would be neither economic nor practical for them to return to the UK, especially if urgent repairs were required. As it was envisaged that it would be unlikely that these great ships would be deployed to the east of the Suez Canal, this facility would not be necessary in the Far East. However, the Mediterranean Fleet would certainly have a battle squadron, so it was decided that a facility should be built at Gibraltar. The result was the excavation of the massive Prince and Princess of Wales Dock, which was opened by their Royal Highnesses in 1907. A dock that was capable of holding 100,000 tons of water, the Mediterranean Fleet dreadnoughts had their own 'garage' on their doorstep.

The Naval Treaties

When what was to become known as the Great War, or the 'war to end all wars', came to an end in 1918, the greater part of the world was exhausted physically, mentally and certainly financially. With the cessation of hostilities, governments were able to take time to look about them and take stock of the appalling harvest reaped in the previous four years. Apart from the dreadful toll in lives, the drain on economies was precariously exorbitant. Either individually or together, governments quickly came to the conclusion that the very last thing that was required was another arms race such as had been experienced in the years before the war; however, in some quarters, plans were already being formulated for huge naval expansion. In the United States the administration of President Woodrow Wilson revealed plans for a US Navy of no fewer than fifty powerful modern battleships to be at sea by the year 1919. Britain, which at this time still commanded the largest and most powerful navy in the world, had plans to build another four battleships and another four battlecruisers, with more battleships to be laid down within a year of the first batch being completed.

In the Far East the Japanese government had authorised the building of eight new battleships and eight new battlecruisers, all greatly more powerful than preceding classes, in what they termed as their 'Eight-Eight' Policy. Very soon work commenced on the first four of these battleships, as well as the first four battlecruisers. In Europe, France and Italy had similar ambitions.

In the United States, however, the Wilson administration had run into difficulties. Not only was public opinion against armed expansion, but the US Congress had, unsurprisingly, completely rejected any such plans. It was appreciated that the enormous cost of building, manning and maintaining a fleet of fifty massive new battleships was totally unsustainable. Furthermore, US public opinion was beginning to swing back to the pre-war non-interventionist policy.

In post-war Britain money was extremely tight and great difficulty would be experienced in stretching the national purse strings to the extent of covering the astronomic cost of new battleship construction. However, there was a problem that had to be faced. Britain had to have new battleships as well as other types of warships to 'keep up with the Joneses'. If America was to have them, Japan was already building them and no doubt France and Italy would be following suit, then it was essential for Britain to maintain the lead they had on all the other navies.

During 1920 Britain had been making arrangements to hold a conference, the subject of which was to be the strategic implications of the Far East and the Pacific. However, the Americans were already beginning to consider this geographical area as their personal backyard, so as soon as they got wind of Britain's intentions they forestalled such plans by calling for a global conference on disarmament.

Thus blossomed the age of the great naval treaties, with the Washington Naval Treaty, which took place from November 1921 to February 1922 under the auspices of the Harding administration, being the forerunner. Britain, USA, France, Italy and Japan, being the victors of the First World War, sat at the table and thrashed out the details of disarmament. Germany, of course, did not appear at this conference, as their building and maintenance limitations had been dealt with by the Treaty of Versailles, which was signed soon after the scuttling of the German High Seas Fleet at Scapa Flow in 1919.

When the Washington Conference broke up in February 1922 after much bartering and arguing, an agreement had been finally reached. Nations were restricted as to the total tonnages they could build: Britain and the USA were allowed 525,000 tons, Japan 315,000 tons and France and Italy 175,000 tons each. With this went the stipulation that capital ships (battleships and battlecruisers) were to be restricted to a maximum of 35,000 tons and to mount guns no larger than 16-inch calibre – a situation with which, it seemed, everyone went away contented.

The letter of the treaty was strictly adhered to in Britain, where in 1921 a new class of 53,909-ton battlecruisers, referred to provisionally as the G3 Type, had been muted. With nine 16-inch 45-calibre guns, they would have been very powerful indeed, but the project, which had been far from popular with the Treasury, was killed outright having barely reached the drawing-board stage as being well in excess of the displacement permitted by the treaty. Equally unpopular with the Treasury was the Admiralty's plan to build four 48,500-ton battleships in 1922. This class, referred to provisionally as 'N' Class, armed with nine 18-inch guns, would have been the most powerful British battleships ever to have been commissioned, but these suffered the same fate as the G3 battlecruisers and barely got to the drawing board. What both of these rejected classes had achieved, however, was to provide great power to Britain's elbow when it had come to bargaining in Washington.

The restrictions laid down by the treaty were due to expire at the end of 1936, so there followed a number of new treaties, all with the intention of extending and/or reiterating the restrictions laid down in Washington. This was the aim of the First and Second London treaties, but there was now dissension in the ranks to the extent that both Japan and Italy withdrew from the conferences and refused to concur, even though the other signatories agreed to be bound by the original terms.

The Treaty's Effect in Britain

Without doubt there were some strange anomalies thrown up by compliance with the Washington Treaty. An extreme example was Britain's Nelson Class, the two ships being launched in 1925. Originally intended to be battlecruisers of 48,000 tons, *Nelson* and *Rodney* had the misfortune to fall afoul of the treaty, which, as we have seen, restricted displacements to 35,000 tons. So they were redesigned as battleships, and in pursuit of weight-saving their appearance developed a most unusual, not to say bizarre, design in battleship terms.

Like bosomly middle-aged matrons, they carried everything before them and sported the longest fo'c'sles ever seen on a warship, with all their main armament mounted on this extraordinary proboscis. The nine 16-inch guns in three triple turrets were all mounted here, with 'B' turret being raised up to superfire over 'A', but the third turret, known as 'X', was mounted behind 'B' turret so that it was able to fire only on

HMS *Nelson, c.* 1925, had a most unusual design. (Author's collection)

The British Home Fleet at Rosyth, Scotland, *c.* 1930. Alongside the jetty (far left) is the unmistakable shape of a Nelson Class forecastle. (Evan Williams)

either beam. None of these big guns could fire astern. With the superstructure situated very far aft and all main armament in front of it, the ships presented an extraordinary truncated appearance. When they joined the fleet their outlandish profiles appealed to the sailors' sense of humour and, hardly surprisingly, they were soon nicknamed the 'Cherry Tree Class' (cut down by Washington).

Having spent her pre-war service carrying out the dreary routine of peacetime duties in the Atlantic and Home fleets, *Nelson* went on to have a lively war, during which she sustained a number of injuries. The first came early, when in December 1939 she had the misfortune to attract a magnetic mine off Loch Ewe, Scotland, requiring her to spend eight months in Portsmouth Dockyard. In September 1941 while escorting a convoy from Gibraltar to Malta she lost an argument with an aerial torpedo and it was back to the dockyard until April 1942. For some time she managed to stay out of trouble in operations in the Mediterranean, which included the landings at Salerno, North Africa and Sicily, and returned to the UK to take part in the Normandy

HMS *Nelson* clearly shows the immense fo'c'sle with 'B' turret superfiring over 'A' turret and 'X' turret tucked in behind 'B' turret. (Luis Photos, Gibraltar)

Landings, in the course of which she suffered severe damage from two magnetic mines in the English Channel. Limping across the Atlantic, she was taken in hand at Philadelphia for repair and was back at sea in time to take part in the final operations against the Japanese in Malaya. Post-war, she served for a short time in the Home Fleet before being sold to the breakers in 1948.

Until the beginning of the war *Rodney* followed much the same pattern. In 1940 she was operational in the Norway campaign, during which she sustained minor damage from a bomb. The following year she was involved in the destruction of the German battleship *Bismark*, after which she went to the Mediterranean with Force H. She, too, covered the landings in North Africa, Sicily and Salerno, and from then on she was employed mainly in bombardment operations until the war's end. Post-war, she was sold off to the breakers in 1948.

HMS *Rodney* with a clear view of her aircraft perched in its catapult on top of 'X' turret. (Author's collection)

Post-Second World War – The Swansong!

With the ending of the Second World War the message was there for all to see – aircraft were the nemesis of the dreadnought no matter how well armed they were, and more especially if they had no air cover to protect their vulnerability, they were child's play. Yet despite this message and others coming from battleship actions in all theatres of the Second World War, Britain was to launch one more dreadnought.

The 52,250-ton *Vanguard*, a single ship mounting eight 15-inch guns in four twin turrets, had been envisaged in 1939 before the outbreak of the war. This time the designers didn't make the mistake of designing her with 16-inch guns as they had in the case of the abandoned Lion Class; indeed, it had finally dawned on the designers

HMS *Vanguard* was the world's last battleship to be built and was considered by many to be the ultimate in battleship beauty. (Author's collection)

that big guns didn't just appear in the builder's yard but had to be manufactured, which was no mean feat. However, it was discovered that in the dim, dark obscurity of numerous Admiralty armament stores depots there were 15-inch guns and turrets aplenty, so this was to be the size of her main armament.

Finally, after numerous additions and alterations to the design occasioned by experiences drawn from the war that was raging, she was laid down in John Brown's Clydebank yard in Scotland in October 1941. Over the following three years a stop-start process evolved as materials became unavailable and then available or some detail of design alteration was absorbed, so it was not until November 1944 that she savoured the salt waters of the Clyde. Even then it was to be another two years before she was completed and commissioned in May 1946, just over four and a half years from the date of the ceremony that saw her laid down.

She was, of course, a dinosaur – but a very beautiful dinosaur! The largest, fastest battleship ever built for the Royal Navy, she was for that matter not only the last British battleship to be built, but the very last battleship in the world to be launched.

She was not destined for old age, but while she was afloat she carved out a quite exciting career. Seldom out of the limelight, she started her short life in a blaze of glory at the end of her commissioning year by being earmarked to act as a royal yacht to convey George VI and the royal family on the first ever royal tour of South Africa. Accordingly, at the end of January 1947, with the royal family ensconced in her luxurious staterooms, she set off for South Africa. The tour lasted for nearly three months, so it was not until May 1947 that she returned to the UK bearing her royal cargo, which she discharged at Portsmouth.

Later that year she was taken in hand at Devonport Dockyard for refitting – a process that was to last until August the following year, and it was while in dockyard hands that she received the news she was to engage in another royal tour, this time taking the king and his family to Australia and New Zealand in January 1949. Sadly, no sooner had she freed herself from dockyard hands and carried out her post-refit trials in the Mediterranean than it was announced that owing to the ill health of His Majesty the tour was postponed indefinitely. With the end of her royal yacht engagements she settled down to become the flagship firstly of the Mediterranean Fleet, and then as the flagship of the Home Fleet back in the UK. She was always a very active ship and for almost all of her career she was a flagship for one admiral or another.

In October 1959 the Admiralty announced that the mighty *Vanguard* was to be scrapped. She was, they said, obsolete and far too expensive to maintain. She was sold to a ship-breaker for the measly sum of £560,000 and a billet was prepared for her at the breakers' yard at Faslane in the Gareloch, Scotland. On 4 August 1960 she was taken in tow at Portsmouth but was obviously not prepared to go quietly. As a final gesture of defiance the very grand lady shook off the tow and slewed across the mouth of the harbour, taking the ground close to a public house. It took five tugs and an hour or more to break her free from the land and resume her last dejected voyage. Five days later she was towed sullenly into her berth in the Gareloch to submit to the searing torture of the breakers' torches.

With her arrival on the naval scene in 1946, the final curtain was descending over the great dreadnought era; there were to be no more built and only those already in existence were to eke out their lives in the latter half of the twentieth century. A number of the battleships of the United States Navy were to outlive *Vanguard* and several of those exist into the twenty-first century around the coasts of the United States as static museum ships. It seems a matter of regret that *Vanguard* could not have ended her days in this mode.

The First American Dreadnoughts

It would be unfair to infer that the American Navy was infected by 'Dreadnought Fever' as it already had pretensions of becoming one of the world's leading navies, and with their advancements in the industrial field the Americans set to with a will building some very powerful vessels.

Their first foray into the dreadnought world came with the launch in 1908 of the two ships of the 17,617-ton South Carolina Class, *Michigan* and *South Carolina*. The Americans had already reached the conclusion that the 'all big-gun' concept was the way ahead. The fact of the matter is that had they prosecuted the building of the South Carolina Class with the same urgency that had seen the launch of *Dreadnought*, it is quite probable it would have been they that were the world's first 'all big-gun battleships' and we might now be talking of South Carolinas rather than dreadnoughts. As it was, the class was subjected to a much more leisurely approach in design and building, so that when they were completed in 1910 they were more technically advanced than *Dreadnought*, with superior armour and a weapons layout that was not surpassed throughout the era of battleships.

They were, however, somewhat slower than the British prototype. Though only slower by 2½ knots, this was sufficient to be telling in a battle situation. *South Carolina* spent most of her life in the Atlantic and Caribbean on coastal patrols of the US, and as a break from that routine in 1913–14 she patrolled the coast of Mexico during the Mexican Revolution, protecting American interests. When America entered the war in 1917 she assumed a training role, introducing new recruits to the naval way of life. Post-war she and her sister were casualties of the Washington Naval Treaty and were broken up in the mid-1920s.

The appearance of these two ships sent a message to the world – particularly to the British – which said loudly and clearly: 'We're the Americans. We're here, we're here to stay and we're damned good – every bit as good as you!' To prove their point they engaged in a positive frenzy of battleship construction as class after class of dreadnoughts followed the South Carolinas.

Contrary to the British battleship building programme, which could see four, six or even eight ships to a class, each of the American classes comprised only two ships, and not until the arrival of the New Mexico Class in 1917 was there a three-ship class. Nonetheless, the two-ship classes came roaring down the slipways one after the other.

USS *South Carolina* – the first of the US Navy's dreadnoughts. Here she shows off the USN's distinctive 'basket' masts. (US Naval History & Heritage Command)

The two 22,060-ton Delaware Class, comprising *Delaware* and *North Dakota*, had been launched in 1909, and were at sea. Armed with ten 12-inch guns, *Delaware* spent all her life in the Atlantic, and when America entered the First World War she deployed to Britain to join the Grand Fleet, joining the 6th Battle Squadron. However, she saw no action during the hostilities and at the end of the war she returned to her home waters to fleet exercises and goodwill visits to foreign ports. A victim of the Washington Treaty, she was broken up in the mid-1920s. Her sister ship, also a victim of the treaty, had a very mundane career, seeing no action whatsoever and never firing a shot in anger. She was present when the USA occupied Veracruz, but when America entered the First World War she remained in American waters in a training role.

The Delawares were followed in 1911 by the two 23,033-ton Florida Class ships, *Florida* and *Utah*, with their ten 12-inch guns and a secondary armament of sixteen 5-inch guns. *Utah* was the first to be launched at the New York Navy Yard

A standard US Naval 12-inch 45-calibre gun. (US Naval History & Heritage Command)

in December 1909, being followed by *Florida* five months later in May 1910, the latter having been built by the New York Shipbuilding Corporation. They were both completed in 1911 and commissioned into the USN. They were present when the US occupied Veracruz during the Mexican Revolution and when the USA entered the First World War in 1917, *Florida* was one of the ships to cross the Atlantic to join Britain's Grand Fleet as a unit of the 6th Battle Squadron, but she saw no action. *Utah* also crossed the Atlantic and spent her time in Bantry Bay, Ireland. On return to the States after the war, they resumed normal peacetime patrols and exercises. In 1924 *Florida* underwent a two-year major refit, rejoining the fleet in 1926. Both ships became victims of the 1930 London Naval Treaty, which resulted in *Florida* being broken up in 1932. *Utah*, on the other hand, remained afloat, although she was reduced to a target in 1931 under the treaty. She was employed training anti-aircraft gunners and it was in

USS *Delaware*, built at Newport News, was competed in 1910. (US Naval History & Heritage Command)

this role that she was in Pearl Harbour when the Japanese attacked. Hit by two aerial torpedoes, she shipped a large amount of water, turned on her side and sank, with sixty-four of her crew being killed. The wreck remains visible under the water and in 1972 a memorial was erected on the shore nearby.

The year 1910 saw the two ships of the 27,243-ton Wyoming Class, *Wyoming* and *Arkansas*, laid down, and by 1912 they were in commission. They were considered a great improvement over their predecessors in several ways, with their armament increased by an additional twin 12-inch turret to twelve 12-inch guns and for the first time in an American vessel they were built with a torpedo bulkhead. For a while it had been muted to arm them with larger 14-inch guns, but this idea was rejected, their manufacture being too complicated at that time. As with a number of other American warships, when they became involved in the First World War in 1917 they were deployed to the UK to join the Grand Fleet battle squadrons.

Apart from a short spell in the Pacific in 1919–21, they spent most of their time in the Atlantic between the wars. *Wyoming* fell afoul of the 1930 London Naval Treaty,

A product of the New York Navy Yard, USS *Florida* was completed in 1911. (US Naval History & Heritage Command)

which saw her reduced to a training role and being slighted of six of her big gun turrets together with her belt armour and anti-torpedo bulges it was in this role that she served throughout the Second World War. In 1944 she was rearmed with a suit of anti-aircraft guns of various types so that she could train prospective gunners in their use. *Arkansas*, on the other hand, was permitted to remain intact by the treaty and so saw extensive service in both the Atlantic and the Pacific. Both vessels were paid off after the war, with *Arkansas* being expended in 1946 as a target and *Wyoming* heading for the breakers' yard the following year.

Designed as an improvement on the previous Wyoming Class, the 28,367-ton New York Class were in commission, with *Texas* commissioning in March 1914 and her sister ship *New York* the following month. These were the first American ships to mount the new 14-inch guns, having ten guns in twin turrets. They were lacking in some respects, however, certainly in the area of an anti-aircraft capability, and there was concern too over the layout of her armour – problems that had to be addressed

Loading drill on one of USS *Florida's* 5-inch guns. (US Naval History & Heritage Command)

later in their careers. For some reason the USN had not followed the general trend of abandoning coal-fired engines in favour of oil, but this class was to be the last of America's coal-burning battleships. Almost immediately on commissioning they were involved in America's occupation of Veracruz, and when the States entered into the First World War they joined other USN battleships reinforcing the British Grand Fleet in the North Sea.

During this conflict *New York*'s claim to fame was that she is thought to have accidentally destroyed an enemy submarine in a collision. When the Second World War broke out in Europe, America remained neutral, and both ships took part in their neutrality patrols of the American east coast. When America finally entered the war these ships had been overtaken by obsolescence and their roles in the conflict were limited to convoy escorts and bombardments for European operations, and then in the Pacific for Iwo Jima and Okinawa. Post-war, *New York* was expended in 1948 as a target, but *Texas* was taken in hand for conversion to a museum ship and remains in that role in the twenty-first century at San Jacinto State Park.

By the time war came in Europe the US Navy had ten dreadnoughts in commission, with a further four already having been laid down. The 28,400-ton Nevada Class,

USS *Arkansas* was to serve throughout the Second World War and, of service to the last, was sunk as a target in 1946. Note the two 'float planes' in their stowage amidships. (US Naval History & Heritage Command)

comprising *Nevada* and *Oklahoma*, were America's first oil-burning Dreadnoughts and were also the first USN ships to mount main armament guns in a triple turret, and were designed with long-range gunnery targets in mind. This showed remarkable forethought on the part of the Americans, especially as other navies – particularly the British – still envisaged long lines of dreadnoughts battering each other to death at comparatively short ranges. When America entered the First World War in 1917 the class was deployed on convoy escorts across the Atlantic, but between the wars they both underwent long refits and modernisations, which stood them in good stead in the Second World War. They were present at Pearl Harbour when the Japanese struck and *Oklahoma* paid the extreme penalty, being sunk at her moorings and taking

USS *Texas*. A veteran of the First World War, she lived to fight in the next great conflict. She is seen here recovering an aircraft at Iwo Jima in 1945. (US Naval History & Heritage Command)

410 of her crew with her when hit by several aerial torpedoes. In 1943 attempts were made to salvage her by righting her and bringing her to the surface, but it was soon realised that her injuries were too great to be repaired and so she was stripped of her guns and superstructure. Post-war she was sold to be broken up. Stubborn to the last, she sank in a storm while in tow for the breakers' yard.

Nevada meanwhile lived on to fight in both the Atlantic and the Pacific and took part in the bombardment of the Normandy beaches in the D-Day operations. Post-war she was considered to be too old and too tired to be of front-line use and was relegated to a target for nuclear and conventional weapons in the mid-1940s, until she was eventually sunk as a target in 1948.

A USN 18-inch torpedo tube. (US Naval History & Heritage Command)

The other ships that had already been laid down prior to the outbreak of the First World War were the 32,567-ton Pennsylvania Class ships *Pennsylvania* and *Arizona*. Both launched in 1915, they fell into the newly coined category of 'super dreadnoughts', having two turrets forward – one superfiring over the other. As an improvement on the previous Nevadas they mounted an extra pair of 14-inch guns, bringing their main armament up to twelve 14-inch guns mounted in four triple turrets. When the United States entered the war in 1917 they were still the USN's newest battleships, but saw only limited service during the hostilities. In the UK there was a serious shortage of oil fuel, so the USN ships that were deployed to join the Grand Fleet were all coal burners – one of the very rare occasions where coal was preferred to oil! Having undergone extensive modernisation in 1921–31 they were ready and able to take part in the Second World War, being deployed to the Pacific, which meant that they were both present when the Japanese treacherously struck at Pearl Harbour. *Arizona* was hit several times and suffered a massive magazine explosion, which sent her to the bottom. Her sister ship fared somewhat better due to the fact that she was docked down at the time of the attack. Sustaining only superficial damage, she lived to fight another day, which she did mainly in the role of a bombarding ship, bringing her twelve 14-inch guns into play. With just two days to go to the cessation of hostilities she sustained a torpedo hit and due to her age she was considered not worth proper repair. With the minimal work carried out on her she was employed in the Bikini Atoll nuclear tests and then finally expended as a target in 1948.

The three-ship 33,000-ton New Mexico Class were laid down during the conflict and launched in 1917. Two of the class were completed before the war's end: *Mississippi*

USS *Mississippi* and a good view of the forward 14-inch twin turret – the sailor on top provides a good guide to the scale. (US Naval History & Heritage Command)

As the last of the New Mexico Class to be commissioned in 1919, USS *Idaho* was too late for the First World War but served throughout the Second World War. (US Naval History & Heritage Command)

in December 1917 and *New Mexico* in May 1918. It was not until March 1919, some months after the Armistice, that the last of the class, *Idaho*, was commissioned.

The twelve 14-inch guns they mounted were similar to those in the preceding Pennsylvania Class but were of an increased calibre (50 as opposed to 45 calibre) and mounted in improved triple turrets. At the same time they sported 'clipper' bows, which were intended to achieve better seakeeping qualities as well as giving them a very modern appearance. Propulsion followed established lines in *Mississippi* and *Idaho* with standard geared turbines, but *New Mexico* broke the mould with electric-drive turbines – not that they made any difference to her speed or range, which was reported as being uniform with others in the class. Between 1931 and 1934 they underwent considerable modifications and refitting, which readied them for the forthcoming conflict. For the duration of the Second World War they operated in the

Pacific theatre – although briefly, in 1941, forming up as Battleship Division 3, they were deployed to the Atlantic in reply to the German threat. However, this left the American fleet in the Pacific considerably weaker than the Japanese. After the attack on Pearl Harbour, when a number of USN battleships were destroyed or put out of action, they were recalled to the Pacific, where they were desperately needed. Here they remained, giving gunfire support to many of the amphibious operations until the Japanese surrender in 1945. Post-war, *New Mexico* and *Idaho* were paid off into the Reserve until they were both broken up at Newark in 1947. *Mississippi* sailed on to become a training and weapons trials ship and it was in this role that she tested the first of the USA's ship-launched guided missiles. Over forty years old, she was finally broken up at Baltimore in 1956.

The design of these early American dreadnoughts was quite distinctive, with their peculiar multi-tubular basket-like masts, a feature that was to last well into the Second World War. However, despite the introduction of the battlecruiser in Britain, the USN was not tempted to dabble in this particular pond, which, as it turned out, was probably greatly to her advantage.

Treaty Restricted Building in the United States

In those countries that had agreed to abide by the treaties, dreadnought building carried on in a rather desultory manner, with the leader in the building stakes being the USA. The three ships of the 33,000-ton New Mexico Class had been laid down during the war and had been launched in 1917. *Mississippi* had been the first to be completed in December 1917, followed by *New Mexico* in 1918 and lastly by *Idaho* in 1919 before the Washington Treaty came into being.

The Tennessee Class, comprising two 33,190-ton battleships, *Tennessee* and *Califoria*, were completed in 1920 and 1921 respectively. They were both to serve in one way or another for forty years, including throughout the Second World War. They eventually kept their appointments with the breakers' torches in 1959.

Post-treaty, two classes were abandoned, the first being the 43,200-ton South Dakota Class. This five-ship class comprising *South Dakota*, *Indiana*, *Montana*, *North Carolina* and *Iowa* had been launched in 1920, but all suffered cancellation in August 1923, the date the Washington Treaty came into operation. The class name was to be resurrected in 1939 when a revised South Dakota Class was laid down.

The years 1920/21 saw America's only venture into battlecruiser building when the 44,638-ton Lexington Class was ordered. However, the venture was short-lived. The class, comprising *Lexington*, *Constellation*, *Saratoga*, *Ranger*, *Constitution* and *United States*, got as far as being launched, but got no further and was cancelled in 1923. The two exceptions to this were *Lexington* and *Saratoga*, which were completed as aircraft carriers.

The Colorado Class was pre-Washington Treaty. At 33,590 tons they would have fitted within the treaty's restrictions anyway, so *Colorado*, *Maryland* and *West Virginia* were all launched and went on to completion in the early 1920s.

The fourth ship of the lass, *Washington*, got as far as being launched, but thereafter work on her ceased. Her hulk rendered an important service to the US Navy when she went out in a blaze of glory as a target in November 1924, having been subjected to hundreds of tons of high explosive hurled at her from the surface, from under the surface and from the air. Her suffering proved to the US Navy that their battleships were under-armoured and required 'triple bottom' protection. With the building of these dreadnoughts America had used up a very large slice of her allowance under the treaty, so no more battleships were built between the wars and the remaining allowance was taken up by other types of warships.

The Tennessee Class dreadnought USS *California* is cheered down the slipway for her first taste of salt water at the New York Navy Yard on 20 November 1919. (US Naval History & Heritage Command)

USS *Montana*, a dreadnought seen under construction at the Mare Island Navy Yard in 1921. She was one of the aborted South Dakota Class, which was abandoned under the Washington Treaty in 1923. (US Naval History & Heritage Command)

USS *Colorado* was the lead ship of the class, which managed to be completed before the Washington Treaty restrictions. (US Naval History & Heritage Command)

Post-Treaty Building in the USA

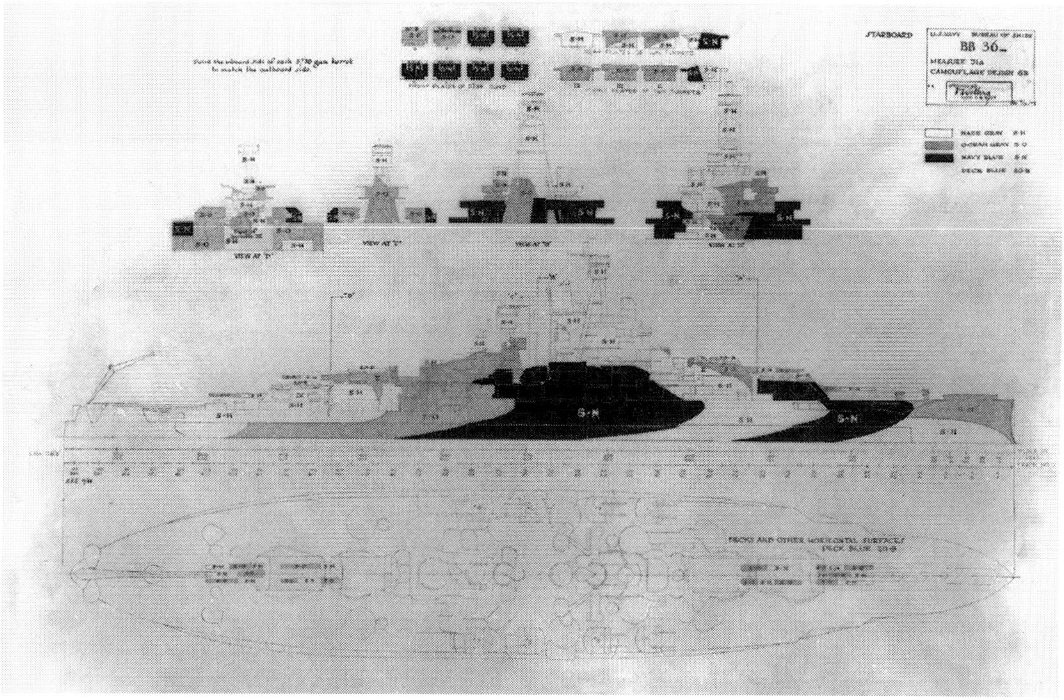

A template for the Dazzle paint employed in the Second World War. Dazzle paint was a sort of camouflage for ships at sea, with the theory being that it broke up the ship's profile, to the confusion of submarines in particular. (US Naval History & Heritage Command)

With the lapse of the treaties, and with indisputable signs that yet another conflict was looming ominously on the European horizon, orders started flowing into the American building yards for all types of ships. The first post-treaty battleships off the drawing board were the 44,377-ton North Carolina Class, comprising the two battleships *North Carolina* and *Washington*. Mounting a main armament of nine 16-inch guns and an armoured belt of between 6 and 12 inches, they were launched in 1940 and completed the following year. Both ships survived the conflict and post-war were paid off and laid up. In 1961 they were considered dispensable and *Washington* was towed away to a breakers' yard, but her sister was given a new lease of life when she was taken in hand for preservation.

Next to trundle down the slipways was the South Dakota Class. The four 44,519-ton ships of this class – *South Dakota*, *Indiana*, *Massachusetts* and *Alabama* – were all launched in 1941, not long before the attack on Pearl Harbour.

By mid-1942 they had all been completed and had donned their war garb. For the most part their war service was to be in the Pacific, and not only did they all survive hostilities but remained in being into the 1960s, albeit in the Reserve, until *South Dakota* and *Indiana* were sold to breakers. The remaining two ships, however, were spared the ignominy of the breakers torches and were taken in hand for preservation. *Alabama* was later added to the National Historic Landmark registry.

An aerial photograph *c.* 1942 showing a supply vessel and two destroyers alongside USS *South Dakota*. (US Naval History & Heritage Command)

Massachusetts had a slightly different passage to preservation. Having been decommissioned in 1947 she was laid up at Portsmouth, Virginia, until, in 1962, she was considered dispensable and was due to be taken away to the breakers. The people of Massachusetts, however, had other ideas. They formed the Massachusetts Memorial Committee and with funds collected persuaded the USN to hand the battleship into their care, with the result being that in 1965 the Massachusetts Museum opened to the public.

USS *Indiana*. Even a mighty dreadnought demanded her people had good sea legs. (US Naval History & Heritage Command)

USS *Massachusetts*. Rescued from the breakers' yard through public subscription by the people of Massachusetts, she was preserved as a museum. (US Naval History & Heritage Command)

With the completion of the Dakota Class, the USN now had six shiny new dreadnoughts, but this was not enough for what was to become the world's largest navy, so the six 57,540-ton ships of the Iowa Class were laid down. In 1942 the *Iowa* and *New Jersey* were launched, having been laid down in 1940. The *Missouri* and *Wisconsin* were laid down in 1941. *Wisconsin* was launched in 1942 but *Missouri* didn't bite into salt water until 1944. The penultimate member of the class, *Illinois*, was laid down in December 1942, but her launching was put off until she was finally cancelled in 1945. The last of the class, *Kentucky*, having been laid down in 1942, was also put on hold. She was finally launched as late as 1950, but work on her ceased and she was sold uncompleted to a breaker in 1958.

The Iowa Class was remarkable for its longevity. The four ships of this class that were completed during, and saw action in, the Second World War, carried on their careers throughout the century, although there were long periods in the Reserve. They continued service well into the twenty-first century before all becoming museum ships based around the USA. In this respect they are still extant.

USS *Missouri* and a huge moment in history – the signing of the Japanese Instrument of Surrender in Tokyo Bay on 2 September 1945. (US Naval History & Heritage Command)

Iowa had a very colourful career, being the largest USN ship ever built. In 1943 she carried President Roosevelt to North Africa on his way to the historic meeting with Winston Churchill and Joseph Stalin at Tehran. After the war she took part in the Korean War, on completion of which she was reduced to the Reserve, where she remained until 1984 when she was brought forward to recommission for operations in the Atlantic and the Pacific, and it was during this commission she suffered an explosion in No. 2 gun turret, which killed forty-seven men and wrecked the turret. She was paid off again in 1990, and was actually stricken from the list, but that was not the end of her. In 1999 she was reinstated and remained on the list until finally, in 2006, at the grand old age of sixty-four, she was gifted out of the USN to the Los Angeles Pacific Battleship Centre. Six years later she was opened to the public as a museum ship.

The engine room of a dreadnought *c.* 1943. (US Naval History & Heritage Command)

A standard 12-inch gun being carefully guided into its housing in a turret. (US Naval History & Heritage Command)

USS *New Jersey* operated in the Pacific in the Second World War and saw action again in the Korean War in 1950–53. In 1955 she was reduced to the Reserve until being brought forward in 1984 and recommissioned. She saw more action in Operation *Desert Storm* in 1991, but was paid off once more the following year. Having been stricken in 1995 she was taken in hand for preservation and became a museum ship at Pearl Harbour, where, in 1998, she was joined by her sister ship *Missouri*. *Wisconsin* was also bound for a career as a museum ship and in 2010 opened her gangways to visitors at Norfolk, Virginia. *New Jersey* was the most decorated battleship in the history of the US Navy, receiving a total of nineteen battle stars.

Yet more dreadnoughts were planned for the USN, and in 1941 the first of the six-ship 34,253-ton Alaska Class, *Alaska*, was laid down, being launched in 1943. In 1942 *Guam* was laid down and she too was launched in 1943, but these were the only ships of the class to be completed and both were broken up in 1961. Of the remainder of the class, *Hawaii* was laid down in 1943 and launched in 1945, but work on her ceased and in an incomplete state she was broken up in 1960. *Philippines*, *Puerto Rico* and *Samoa* all failed to reach the laying down process and were officially cancelled in 1943.

A class of giant 70,500-ton battleships was envisaged in the early 1940s ostensibly in reply to the Japanese Yamato Class. This was the Montana Class, which was to comprise *Montana*, *Ohio*, *Maine*, *New Hampshire* and *Louisiana*, but they got no further than the drawing board and when they were officially cancelled in 1943, it signalled the end of dreadnought building in the United States of America.

French Dreadnoughts

France, which was to become a protagonist in the forthcoming First World War, commenced a dreadnought building programme in 1910 when the first of her three pre-war classes were laid down. The four ships of the 25,579-ton Courbet Class – *Courbet*, *France*, *Jean Bart* and *Paris* – were launched in 1911/12. Close on their heels, in 1913 came the three ships of the 26,180-ton Bretagne Class, *Bretagne*, *Lorraine* and the ill-fated *Provence*.

The last French partial pre-war build was the 25,230-ton Normandie Class, *Bearn*, *Flandre*, *Gascoigne*, *Languedoc* and *Normandie*, which were launched in 1914 with the exception of *Languedoc*, which was launched in 1916. *Bearn* was withdrawn from the class for conversion to an aircraft carrier and as such was relaunched in 1920.

In 1912 France had thoughts of building the impressive 29,000-ton four-ship Lyon Class, comprising *Duquesne*, *Lille*, *Lyon* and *Tourville*, but the planned construction was abandoned due, mainly, to the time it would have taken to design and manufacture the required 13.5-inch guns.

A very splendid tabletop model of *Dunkirque* in the Musée National de la Marine at Toulon, France. (Author's Collection)

Richelieu eventually joined the Allies in 1942 and served with the British Eastern Fleet. (Author's collection)

The Dunkerque Class, comprising *Dunkerque* and *Strasbourg*, was launched in the late 1930s and the ships were completed respectively in 1937 and 1938. They saw little or no service in the Second World War and were ignominiously scuttled in 1942.

The last class of dreadnoughts to be built for the French Navy appeared in 1939 when the 49,850-ton *Richelieu* was launched, followed the following year by her sister ship *Jean Bart*. Originally there were to be four vessels in the class, but sister ships *Clemencaeu* and *Gascoigne* failed to reach the launching stage. *Richelieu* wasn't quite completed when France surrendered to the Germans and was quickly deployed to Dakar, Senegal, West Africa, where she was the target of a number of British attacks. However, she survived and in 1942 joined the Allies. Refitted in the USA she served with the British Eastern Fleet late in the war and was broken up in 1964.

Jean Bart fled to Casablanca when France capitulated and it was here that she had the misfortune to be caught up in the Allied invasion of North Africa, thereby suffering a number of hits from bombs and 15-inch shells. She remained inoperative until 1946, when she was taken in hand for completion work. Finally emerging in May 1955, she took part in the 1956 Suez Campaign, and after a spell in the Mediterranean as a gunnery tender she was paid off in 1961 to be hulked at Toulon until the breakers welcomed her in 1970.

Germany Enters the Dreadnought Race

As mentioned earlier, Germany, although having the shipbuilding capacity, was not quite up to the mark in the technological field, but nonetheless she set out on an energetic building programme driven by a fiercely Anglophobic kaiser. This was a programme that was soon to bear fruit, when in 1906 the first of her dreadnoughts, the lead ship of the Deutschland Class, the 14,218-ton *Deutschland*, roared down the slipway of Germaniawerft Schichau-Werke at Wilhelmshaven, to be followed the following year by sister ships *Hannover* and *Pommern*. In 1908, they were followed by the final pair of the class, *Schlesien* and *Schleswig Holstein*. In a sense, the class was caught between two stools in that they were considered by some to be pre-dreadnoughts in their design, and by others as fully paid-up dreadnoughts owing to the fact that their launch dates were post-*Dreadnought*. However, there is no doubt that in line with all the rest of the world's pre-dreadnoughts they were immediately reduced to obsolescence even before their launch. Obsolete they may have been, but they still served with the High Seas Fleet in the First World War and played a part at the Battle of Jutland, during which *Pommern* was torpedoed and sunk. Post-war the Versailles Treaty allowed Germany to retain a number of old battleships for the purpose of coastal defence and the four remaining ships of the class were included in this provision.

Meanwhile, also in Wilhelmshaven, another class was being launched, and in 1907 the four 21,000-ton battleships of the Nassau Class – *Nassau*, *Westfalen*, *Rheinland* and *Posen* – tasted the saltiness of the Baltic waters. Ostensibly these ships were to be a response to *Dreadnought*, but they lacked parity in a number of areas. Their main armament comprised 11-inch guns as opposed to the British 12-inch and they were somewhat slower due to the German policy of retaining vertical triple-expansion engines rather than the faster, more modern turbines. This resulted in the class being at least two knots slower than their British counterparts, but nevertheless they were welcomed into the Imperial Navy and together the four ships formed the 2nd Division of the High Seas Fleet's 1st Battle Squadron. In 1916 they took part in the Battle of Jutland as the 2nd Battle Squadron, lending the weight of their 11-inch guns to the German firepower and emerged from the battle relatively unscathed. At the end of the war they were taken by the Allies as war prizes and sent to the breakers.

Following on from the Nassaus, there was a frenzy of building that saw a class of battleships launched almost every year leading up to the First World War, each class a degree bigger and better than the last as German shipbuilding knowledge expanded.

In 1908–09, the three-funnelled 25,200-ton Helgoland Class, comprising *Helgoland*, *Ostfriesland*, *Thuringen*, and *Oldenburg*, was launched. This was a class that to a degree was an improvement on their predecessors, being larger and armed with 12-inch guns. They were still slower, however, thanks to the designers hanging on to the vertical triple-expansion method of propulsion. This meant they had a top speed of just a shade over 20 knots, but this was still an improvement over the Nassaus. In commission they formed a unit in the 1st Division of the 1st Battle Squadron and saw action in the Battle of Riga, a 1915 action involving the High Seas Fleet against the Russian Baltic Fleet, and also took part in the action at the Battle of Jutland the following year. Despite surviving the war they were not part of the dejected German fleet that sailed into internment in November 1918, but when those unfortunate vessels scuttled themselves in Scapa Flow the Helgolands were ceded to the Allies as war reparation: *Ostfriesland* went to the USN and was expended as a target in a demonstration of air power in 1921; *Helgoland* was allocated to Britain and was broken up in 1921 and *Oldenburg* travelled to the Far East to be handed over to the Japanese and broken up in 1921; and *Theuringen* went to the French, who used her as a target before sending her to a breakers' yard in 1923.

After a little breathing space, the third class of German dreadnoughts built for the Imperial German Navy, the five 27,000-ton ships of the Kaiser Class, comprising the impressively named *Friedrich Der Grasse*, *Kaiser*, *Kaiserin*, *Konig Albert* and *Prinzregent Luitpold* were launched in 1910–11. These ships, each mounting a main armament of ten 12-inch guns, were the first to be built with turbine engines, which propelled them at 21 knots, bringing them up to the existing Dreadnought mark regarding speed. As another 'first' for the Imperial Navy they were the first to employ super-firing guns. During the First World War they formed the 6th Division of the High Seas Fleet's 3rd Battle Squadron and took part in a number of High Seas Fleet operations and four of them were present at the Battle of Jutland (*Konig Albert* was docked down at the time). During the battle *Kaiser* sustained damage from three hits by heavy-calibre shells while the others remained unscathed. In October 1917 they were in the Baltic and took part in the German occupation of the West Estonian Archipelago. They were with the High Seas Fleet to the bitter end when, in November 1918, the fleet surrendered to the Allied navy to be interned in Scapa Flow and came to a sad end when scuttled by their own people on 21 June 1919.

Next to join the German fleet was the pre-First World War four-ship 29,000-ton Konig Class – *Konig*, *Grosser Kurfurst*, *Markgraf* and *Kronprinz* – three of which were launched in 1913, with the last one, *Kronprinz*, entering the water the following year, a few months before the outbreak of the war. An improvement on the Kaiser Class, with their ten 12-inch guns and three steam turbines, which allowed them to steam at a shade over 21 knots, they acted as a unit of the High Seas Fleet, forming the 5th Division of the 3rd Battle Squadron throughout the war. The improvements on the previous class comprised the guns being mounted in five twin turrets, one forward and two aft, with one superfiring over the other and two that had been intended to be wing turrets in a zig-zag formation, but this idea was subsequently abandoned. In preference one turret was moved forward to superfire over the existing forward turret while the other was mounted on the centre line amidships in such a way that it was able to fire astern or on the broadside but not forward. These ships took part in the Battle of Jutland, providing the vanguard for the German line, and in a number of other High Seas Fleet operations. Surviving the war, they were among the ships that surrendered to the Allies in November 1918 for internment at Scapa Flow and suffering an ignominious end when the German Fleet was ordered by their flag officer, Rear Admiral Lugwig von Reuter, to scuttle.

These were the last of Germany's pre-war-built ships as two of the projected four-ship 31,690-ton Bayern Class, *Bayern* and *Baden*, which had been laid down before hostilities commenced, were not actually launched until 1915. Their sister ships in the class, *Sachsen*, which was laid down in April 1914, and *Wurttemburg*, which was laid down in January 1915, are in some lists categorised as being in a class of their own. Be that as it may, after their launch in 1916 and 1917 respectively it was patently obvious that the German Navy was not in any shape to cope with more new-build ships, so neither vessel was ever completed and remained as hulks until being taken to the breakers' yards in 1921. The completed ships, *Bayern* and *Baden*, led fairly unremarkable war careers, having been completed too late for Jutland and

SMS *Konig*, c. 1913. Lead ship of the Konig Class, she took part in a number of operations with the High Seas Fleet, including the Battle of Jutland in 1916, during which she sustained a number of hits from the British big guns but survived to tell the tale. She was with the German High Seas Fleet, which surrendered to the Allies in 1918 and was one of those that scuttled in Scapa Flow on 21 June 1919. (Author's collection)

Kronprinz Wilhelm, c. 1914. Starting life as just plain *Kronprinz*, *Wilhelm* was added in January 1918. She was another of the class that was with the German High Seas Fleet that surrendered to the Allies in 1918 and was one of those scuttled in Scapa Flow on 21 June 1919. (Author's collection)

other High Seas Fleet operations. *Bayern* at least saw some action in Operation *Albion*, which saw the Russian Navy ousted from the Gulf of Riga in October 1917. It was during this operation that she suffered heavy damage from a mine, which necessitated her struggling back to Kiel to be repaired. Both vessels were with the interned fleet in Scapa Flow when ordered to scuttle. *Bayern* carried out this order successfully, but *Baden* was prevented from sinking by her British guards who ran her aground, thus enabling her to end her days in 1921 as a target. The scuttled *Bayern* was raised in 1934 and the wreck was broken up.

There was another very ambitious building programme in Germany's locker at this time, which envisaged a powerful battleship class named, provisionally, the L20A Class. These ships were to weigh in at no less than 48,700 tons and would have been bristling with weapons: eight 16.5-inch, twelve 5.9-inch, eight 3.5-inch or 4.1-inch and three 23.6-inch or 27.6-inch torpedo tubes. Their armour was to be up to 13.8-inches thick making them formidable indeed. They were projected to be built in 1918 and would have been not only very powerful but aesthetically very elegant vessels, but the progression of the war meant they were destined never to leave the drawing board.

In the 3rd Squadron of the High Seas Fleet at the Battle of Jutland, SMS *Markgraf* was one of the unfortunate ships that suffered an ignominious end when scuttled at Scapa Flow in June 1919. (Author's collection)

Battlecruisers of the German Navy

Kaiser Wilhelm II was very conscious of Germany's numerical inferiority with the hated English Navy and to assuage some of this he thrust the Kaiserliche Marine into a programme of battlecruiser building. Totally ignoring their vulnerability he insisted that these vessels should be capable of standing in the line of battle alongside the battleships when, in fact, their role should have been as scouts for the main battle fleet, attacking and destroying scouts of an opposing fleet. Nevertheless, in accordance with the kaiser's demands, the building programme commenced.

In 1909 shipbuilders Blohm & Voss of Hamburg launched the 21,700-ton *Von Der Tann*. This single ship was the forerunner of the German battlecruiser programme and was also among the first of the kaiser's capital ships to employ turbines for propulsion. When she was launched it made Admiral Fisher in his London Admiralty office sit up and take notice for, although she was more lightly armed than Britain's latest Invincible Class, mounting only 11-inch guns to their 12-inch weapons, to offset this the German ship was better protected, carrying a heavier armour than any of the British battlecruisers. Additionally, with her turbines coming in to play she was faster than anything in any other fleet in the world, with a capability of reaching at least 27 knots. Britain's pride and joy, the Invincible Class, could reach a shade over 25 knots at a push.

Von Der Tann was to have a very busy war, including action in a number of bombardments of the English coastline and a major role in the 1916 Battle of Jutland, in the opening stage of which she completely destroyed the British battlecruiser *Indefatigable*, hitting her with a salvo of three 11-inch shells that plunged through the flimsy deck armour and smashed into her vitals. Forced out of the line, *Indefatigable* received another salvo from *Von Der Tann*, with the result being that she completely disintegrated. There were only two survivors out of a ship's company of 1,017. *Von Der Tann* survived the war but her unfortunate end came as one of the ships scuttled at Scapa Flow in 1919. The wreck was raised in 1930 and broken up at Rosyth, Scotland.

Blohm & Voss remained very busy and in 1910 launched the first of the two 25,300-ton Moltke Class. The lead ship, *Moltke*, was launched in the April of that

Von Der Tann was Germany's first battlecruiser. At Jutland she completely destroyed the British battlecruiser *Indefatigable* but was herself to meet a sad end by being scuttled at Scapa Flow in 1919. (Author's collection)

year, followed eleven months later in March 1911 by her sister *Goeben*. The lead ship followed a fairly conventional path through the First World War, being involved in a number of actions with the High Seas Fleet, which included the battles of Dogger Bank, Jutland and Riga. Having safely negotiated hostilities, she too was one of those that met their end being scuttled in Scapa Flow in 1919. Her wreck was raised in 1927 and broken up at Rosyth.

Her sister ship, *Goeben*, however, led a much more unconventional life. By the outbreak of the war she had been deployed to the Mediterranean in company with the light cruiser *Breslau*, and the British were acutely aware of the fact. There followed an extensive operation to track down the two ships and destroy them, but they turned out to be too slippery for the British Mediterranean Fleet and fled eastwards into the well-fortified Dardanelles. Safe in the haven of Constantinople, they were turned over to the Turkish Navy and became a thorn in the side of the Allies throughout the war, becoming another 'Fleet in Being', much as the *Tirpitz* was to be in the Second World War. Snug in their berths in Constantinople, not only did they help to persuade the Ottoman Empire to throw in its lot with the Germans, but they effectively sealed off the Bosphorus, preventing the Russian Black Sea Fleet from entering the Mediterranean and equally preventing an Allied attempt to force that area. Subsequent to the war the new Turkish government was permitted to retain the battlecruiser and she remained on Turkey's active list for many years until finally paying off at the end of 1950. Considered by some to be worth preserving, she was offered to the West German government in 1963 but no takers could be found to carry out the project. All else having failed, she made her way to the breakers' yard in 1971 at the age of sixty.

In the run-up to the First World War battlecruiser building went on apace. The 28,100-ton *Seydlitz* was another Blohm & Voss built ship and was launched in 1912. Completed and commissioned in 1913, she had an interesting and even exciting war. She took part in the Battle of Dogger Bank, during which she sustained severe damage when she was hit on the after turret by a 13.5-inch shell from HMS *Lion* and was lucky not to be destroyed. At the Battle of Jutland she again sustained serious damage, being hit no fewer than twenty-one times by heavy-calibre shells. To compound her injuries she was also hit by a torpedo, which resulted in her taking in several thousand tons of water. Through heroic efforts on the part of her crew she managed to gain the safety of a German harbour and was taken in hand for extensive repairs. On her credit side in the initial actions of the battle she and her consort battlecruiser *Derfflinger* had, with concentrated fire, sunk the British battlecruiser HMS *Queen Mary* in a matter of seconds. *Seydlitz*'s end came when she was scuttled in Scapa Flow in 1919.

In 1913 the two ships of the 30,700-ton Derfflinger Class, *Derfflinger* and *Lutzow*, were launched but were not commissioned until hostilities had commenced. *Derfflinger* was present at the Battle of Dogger Bank and again saw action at Jutland. Surviving the war she was sent to the bottom at Scapa Flow by her own people in 1919.

Lutzow, however, failed to survive the war. Having been commissioned in 1915 she took part in the German battlecruiser attack on Yarmouth on the east coast of England, but subsequently taking part in the Battle of Jutland in 1916 she came under heavy fire from the British ships and was sunk.

The last battlecruiser to be built was the 31,000-ton *Hindenburg*, which, despite being laid down in 1913, wasn't launched at Wilhelmshaven until 1915 due to the exigencies of the war. Some historians would have her as the third ship of the Derfflinger Class while others classify her as a single ship. Without a doubt there were a lot of similarities with the Derfflingers, but there were also many differences that could justify her being in a class of her own. For example, she mounted the same number of 12-inch guns as her predecessors, but they were mounted in a much upgraded turret, which gave them a greater range. At the same time she was larger and faster than the other two and overall she was built to a slightly modified design. Her propulsion, comprising four-shaft Parsons turbines, gave her a speed of 26.6 knots, which was achieved in no small way by her extra length and finer lines aft.

Seydlitz sustained serious damage at the Battle of Dogger Bank in 1915 and again the following year at Jutland. (Author's collection)

Despite all these advantages she had a very disappointing war, not being completed and commissioned until May 1917 – too late for a major fleet action, meaning she was limited to acting as flagship to the 1st Scouting Group for a few small fleet operations. Inevitably she was part of the German High Seas Fleet, seeing her crossing the North Sea into internment in Scapa Flow and suffering the same fate as the rest of the fleet when they were scuttled. Her wreck was raised in 1930 to be towed away to the breakers' yard.

As Britain's closest rival, Germany had fifteen dreadnoughts, another five under construction, four battlecruisers, with another three building, and twenty-two pre-dreadnoughts, but she could also rely on the Austro-Hungarians as allies, who were able to provide another three dreadnoughts with three more building. Although they had no battlecruisers, they could muster six pre-dreadnoughts.

There were three more ambitious classes projected by the Kaiserliche Marine, the first of which was the four-ship 36,000-ton Mackensen Class, and all four – *Mackensen*, *Graf Spee*, *Prinz Eitel Friedrich* and *Furst Bismark* – were laid down in 1915.

One of Germany's successful battlecruisers, *Derfflinger* fought a very active war only to be scuttled ignominiously at Scapa Flow in 1919. (Author's collection)

The first two got as far as being launched in 1917 but then all work stopped and their uncompleted hulls went to the breakers' yards in the early 1920s. The third ship was finally launched post-war in 1920 simply to allow it to be towed away to the breakers. Fourth of the class, *Furst Bismarck*, never even got to the launching stage and her rusting frames were broken up on the slipway in 1920.

A 38,500-ton class provisionally named the Ersatz Yorck Class was projected and one, the *Ersatz Yorck* herself, was laid down in 1916, but that was as far as the class progressed. No others were laid down and all work ceased on the *Yorck*, with her being broken up at a later stage.

The final gasp of this programme was the projected three-ship 35,720-ton 'P' Class, which were provisionally named *O*, *P* and *Q*, but with the intervention of the war these vessels were never laid down and died on the drawing boards.

Germany Prepares for Another Conflict

The post-First World War Versailles Treaty had certainly cramped Germany's style in the shipbuilding stakes. Curbed by the treaty but ambitious in the matter of rebuilding her navy, Germany's shipbuilding became quite confusing. The treaty laid down, in no uncertain terms, that there was a restriction to a maximum of 10,000 tons; however, where there is a will there is a way. 'Cruisers' was a word that often disguised what were, in effect, small battlecruisers. This proved to be the case with the building of the three Deutschland Class ships, *Deutschland*, *Admiral Graf Spee* and *Admiral Scheer*. In pure dreadnought terms they were neither fish, flesh nor fowl and were quite literally in a class of their own. Nominally, in accordance with the treaty, they were under 10,000 tons but by the time they were completed, receiving their full load, they reached 16,280 tons – over one and a half times the treaty's limit. Cruisers they were called, but at that displacement plus a main armament of six 11-inch guns and a top speed of 28.5 knots, they were something very much more than cruisers. By comparison, the Royal Navy's heaviest cruisers, the Kent Class, had a displacement of 13,450 tons, a main armament of eight 8-inch guns and a speed of 31.5 knots. The Germans had designed this class specifically to be able to outgun any cruiser fast enough to catch them and only a few of the battlecruisers in the British and French Navies were fast enough and sufficiently heavily armed to hold them at bay. Small wonder, then, that very early on they were to become known in British circles as 'pocket battleships', but remained classified as heavy cruisers despite the 'pocket battleship' tag.

In terms of 100 per cent battleships, however, Germany produced some truly magnificent vessels. In 1936 came the birth of the two 38,000-ton Scharnhorst Class ships. The issue becomes a little confusing as in some lists they are referred to as the 'Scharnhorst Class' and in others as the 'Gneisenau Class'. Confusion reigns because although *Scharnhorst* was the first ship to be launched, her sister ship was the first to be laid down and commissioned. Both ships were completed well in time for the outbreak of the war and strictly speaking these were the first 'capital ships', either battleships or battlecruisers, built by Germany after the First World War. For a main armament they mounted nine 11-inch guns, which was a cause of some concern in the Kreigsmarine and there were plans to rearm them with 15-inch guns – plans that never materialised. *Gneisenau* was heavily damaged during an air raid on Kiel in late 1942 and was taken in hand there for repair while *Scharnhorst* was deployed to northern waters to join the battleship *Tirpitz* in disrupting Allied convoys to Russia. *Scharnhorst*, having ventured out with several destroyers on a convoy-raiding mission, was intercepted by a British force and in the ensuing action was sunk by the battleship *Duke of York* in what became known as the Battle of North Cape on Boxing Day 1943. This was such a heavy blow to the Kreigsmarine that repair and rearming work on her sister ship was abandoned, but she had one last service to render, which came at Gotenhafen in 1945 when the hulk was sunk as a blockship.

The year 1939 saw a frenzy of German dreadnought launching. The 'Big Beasts' of the German Navy, the two ships that became world famous and were to give the Allies the greatest headaches, were both launched in 1939. The Bismark Class comprised the two ships *Bismark*, of 50,300 tons, and *Tirpitz*, of 52,600 tons. Their main armament of eight 15-inch guns supported by a profusion of smaller weapons made them very formidable protagonists indeed. Such was the charisma of these two ships that the destruction of *Bismark* in May 1941 brought about by the enormous efforts of the Royal Navy has been the subject of numerous books and at least one film.

Operation *Rheinubung* was *Bismark*'s one and only venture into war activity. It was designed to send her out into the Atlantic to cause disruption and mayhem to the vital convoys sailing from the USA to Britain. Unfortunately for her she was spotted by Norwegian agents as she sailed along the Norwegian coast and the information was quickly relayed to London, with the Admiralty dispatching the brand new battleship *Prince of Wales*, still with dockyard workers onboard, and the battlecruiser *Hood* to northern waters to intercept her. They met up with the German battleship in the Denmark Strait and there followed a short, sharp action that proved the formidable strength of the *Bismark*. A salvo from her huge 15-inch guns plunged down through *Hood*'s weakly protected decks and completely destroyed her. Only three men survived the sinking of the Royal Navy's pride and joy. *Prince of Wales*, coming under fire, sustained damage and circumspectly withdrew out of range to take up a shadowing role. There followed a three-day hunt, during which the Royal Navy was in a sweat of activity. The Admiralty called in ships from as far afield as the South Atlantic and Mediterranean to join in the hunt for the German ship and eventually they caught up with her. To the disbelief of the German high command, the mighty *Bismark* was sent to the bottom by a conglomeration of battleships, cruisers, destroyers and aircraft.

There remained *Tirpitz*, a huge headache for more than another three years. Determined that she would never face the destructive situation that had been the fate of her sister ship, she was deployed to the northern Norwegian waters in 1942 where she became the epitome of a 'fleet in being' – a term to describe a ship or fleet that presents a threat. It doesn't have to *do* anything, it just has to be there. *Tirpitz* was in Alten Fjord in northern Norway where she lay in wait, for the most part happily moored inside a protective screen, but the fact that she was there was always a threat to the Russian convoys, which were obliged to pass not overly far to the north between Norway and the Arctic ice fields on their way to and from Russia. Therefore the Allies were forced to fortify the convoys to a much greater extent, which usually meant having a squadron of heavy ships – battleships, battlecruisers etc. – stationed in fairly close proximity to the convoy just in case *Tirpitz* came out. This was of extreme nuisance value in tying up valuable capital ships and men purely on the off-chance that she left her cosy berth.

The Royal Navy employed enormous efforts to be rid of this threat. There was an attack on her by midget submarines, by the Fleet Air Arm and by the Royal Air Force (RAF). Attack after attack was launched, all of which failed dismally, until finally in November 1944 RAF Lancaster bombers managed to hit her with three 5-ton earthquake Tallboy bombs, while several more landed close by. This was, finally, enough to damage her sufficiently for her to capsize, and that was the end of this great ship until she was broken up between 1948 and 1957.

There was a German plan for a six-ship, 62,497-ton class of battleships to be built in 1939. Known provisionally as 'H' Class, they were unnamed and known simply as *H*, *J*, *K*, *L*, *M* and *N*. *H* and *J* got as far as being laid down in June and July 1939 by Blom & Voss of Hamburg and A. G. Weser of Bremen respectively, but then all work ceased. Both keels were broken up within weeks and none of the others were laid down.

'Dreadnought Fever' Spreads to Japan

In the great flurry of activity created by 'Dreadnought Fever', one of the quickest countries off the mark was Japan. Their shipyards quickly adapted to the new format and produced some formidable vessels. The first ships off the stocks, the *Satsuma* and *Aki* of the 20,100-ton Satsuma Class, had been ordered as far back as 1904 as pre-dreadnoughts, but by the time they were launched in 1907 they had been sufficiently modified to be classified as 'semi-dreadnoughts'.

The first true dreadnought of the Japanese Navy appeared in 1910 with the launch of *Kawachi,* the first of the two-ship 21,443-ton Settsu Class, and this was followed the following year by her sister ship *Settsu*.

In 1914 the first of the two-ship 35,000-ton Fuso Class, *Fuso,* was launched by the Kure Naval Yard, but her sister ship *Yamashiro* was obliged to wait for her launching until the First World War was well underway in 1915. By the outbreak of the First World War the Imperial Japanese Navy (IJN) had four modern dreadnought battleships, with three more being built.

The Ise Class battleships were laid down during the First World War. First off the slipway was *ISE* in 1916 followed a year later by sister ship *Hyuga*. Both ships were active in the Second World War and survived for quite some time, before being sunk during the closing stages of the conflict. Both ships went to the bottom of the Pacific in July 1945.

Japan was one of the very few countries to go down the battlecruiser road so that by 1914 the IJN had two battlecruisers in commission with two more completed and commissioned in 1915, but there were no more building. The 32,300T Kongo Class was their first sortie into this field and the first of these, the *Kongo,* was launched in May 1912 to be followed later in the year by the second of the class, *Hiei*. *Kongo* was the last Japanese warship to be built outside Japan, being a product of Vickers of Barrow-in-Furness.

The following year saw the third and fourth of the class, *Kirishima* and *Haruna*, launched, and it was these last two that were not completed until 1915. They were the world's first ships to mount the 14-inch 45-calibre guns in four twin turrets, which made them at the time of launch the heaviest armed ships in the world. In the late 1920s/early 1930s they underwent massive reconstruction, including adding extra

The power of a battleship's searchlights. (Evan Williams)

armour, to the extent that they were re-classified as 'fast battleships'. The lead ship of this class, *Kongo,* is worthy of a mention in her own right. On 21 November 1944 she became the only Japanese battleship to be sunk by a submarine in the Second World War when she ran afoul of the American submarine USS *Sealion*. At the same time, she had the distinction to be the last battleship in history to be sunk by submarine. Tellingly, all other Japanese battleship losses were the result of air attack.

There were two other 'battlecruisers' in commission in 1914. These were the two 13,970-ton ships of the Tsukuba Class, *Tsukuba* and *Ikoma*. These two vessels were something of 'white elephants', having been launched earlier in the century as heavy cruisers, each mounting eight 12-inch guns. However, in 1912 they were upgraded to battlecruisers despite being slower and more lightly armed than their German and British counterparts.

Japan Rejects the Treaties

In terms of shipbuilding technology Japan reached her zenith in this age and is capable of producing beautifully designed and executed vessels. In pursuance of their programme for the expansion of the Imperial Japanese Navy (IJN) they had adopted what they termed as the Eight-Eight Policy, that is to say eight battleships and eight battlecruisers. However, like other nations their building programme was brought up short by the Washington Treaty.

The Amagi Class of battlecruisers was a good example. These four ships, *Amagi*, *Akagi*, *Atago* and *Takao*, each of 47,000 tons fully loaded, would have been a great asset to the IJN, but the treaty said otherwise. All had been laid down in 1920/21, so two vessels, *Atago* and *Takao*, were broken up on the slipways. However, the treaty allowed that, in some circumstances, hulls already under construction could be converted to aircraft carriers, so the remaining two were earmarked for conversion. Unfortunately Mother Nature took a hand in proceedings and while under conversion in 1923 an earthquake damaged *Amagi*'s hull so badly that she was declared a wreck and scrapped. That left the sole survivor of the class, *Akagi*, which, duly completed as a carrier, served in the Pacific in the Second World War, including taking part in the infamous raid on Pearl Harbour in December 1941, until finally being sunk at the Battle of Midway in June 1942.

The Washington Treaty put paid to two more of Japan's planned classes. The 48,600-ton four-ship K.11 Class, planned in 1921, had two named *K.11* and *Owari*, while the other two were still known simply as Numbers 11 and 12. The class was abandoned before a hammer or a welder could operate and a similar fate applied in 1921 to the Number 13 Class of 47,500-ton battlecruisers that was being progressed. Before the ships could be laid down the class was cancelled in November 1923 without even having been named, being known simply as Numbers 13, 14, 15 and 16.

Only marginally less unfortunate were the two 44,200-ton battleships of the Tosa Class. Laid down in 1920 and launched at the end of 1921, these two ships immediately ran afoul of the Washington Treaty. One, *Kaga*, was completed as an aircraft carrier, but her sister ship *Tosa* was cancelled under treaty restrictions. Nevertheless, the uncompleted hull was of further service to the IJN when it was subjected to experiments

IJN *Nagato* survived the Second World War and was finally sunk as a target ship for the US Navy's nuclear weapons tests. Note the unusual bent funnel. (Author's collection)

designed to test the strength of the armour scheme. Having served its purpose, the hulk was finally scuttled in the Bungo Channel between the islands of Kyushu and Shukoku in August 1925.

Inevitably the Japanese became totally disenchanted with international treaties and were unable to accept that Washington could have placed such stringent restrictions on the expansion of their navy. There was fierce opposition to what was considered humiliating pressure from foreigners curtailing their ability to expand their fleet, and there were many who demanded unconditional expansion. Their voices grew more and more vociferous until, eventually, their stridency won the day and this set Japan on an independent building programme.

During the First World War, the two battleships of the 38,500-ton Nagato Class, *Nagato* and *Mutsu,* had been laid down, but their completion dragged on for several years. The lead ship, *Nagato,* was finally completed in 1920, having spent over three years on the stocks, and her sister ship *Mutsu* was finally completed in November 1921.

Both vessels soldiered on to serve in the Second World War, where *Mutsu* came to an unhappy end, having seen comparatively little action during the conflict, with the exception of a small part in the Battle of Midway and in the Battle of the Eastern Solomons – both of which took place in 1942. She was despatched back to Japan in early 1943 and while at anchor in the June of that year one of her after magazines mysteriously exploded, sinking the ship, killing 1,121 crew and several people who were visiting the ship. The IJN carried out an investigation, concluding that the explosion was an act of sabotage by a disgruntled crew member. Her sister, *Nagato*, survived the war to perform a useful service to the USN when, in 1946, she became a target for nuclear weapons tests and was sunk.

To compliment Germany's 'Great Beasts' of the Bismark Class, Japan now proceeded to build her own fearsome vessels. Originally planned as a class of four huge 73,000-ton battleships, they put even the Bismarks, with their eight 15-fifteen guns, in the shade. The four Yamato Class, each with a crew of 2,767 men, were to mount a massive main armament of nine 18.1-inch guns supported by twelve 6.1-inch, twelve 5-inch, twenty-four .98-inch AA guns and a further four .52-inch AA guns. The huge 18.1-inch guns were capable of hurling a 3,220-lb (approximately 1.4-ton) shell. Firing full broadsides she could hurl 30,000 tons of high explosive over a distance of 26 miles, a mighty armament indeed and, as could be expected, there was impressive armour to protect all this firepower. The gun turrets had no less than 26 inches of armour, 16 inches on the ship's sides and 8 inches on her decks. Not only should they have been unapproachable, but unsinkable as well!

Of the four monsters that had been planned, the building of one of their number was halted not long after her launch in 1940 and the incomplete hull was broken up in 1942. Another, *Shinano*, was completed as an aircraft carrier with the remaining two completed as planned to become the largest battleships, not only during the war, but

Yamato – Japan's monster of the sea. Her massive 18-inch guns were capable of hurling 30,000 tons of high explosive over 26 miles. (Author's collection)

the largest ever to be built worldwide. In the mid-1940s the Americans had planned to build a class of 70,000-ton battleships, but by this time it had become obvious that battleships were in their twilight years and so the project was abandoned. A fertile imagination could picture the spectacle of a battle between the Yamatos and two of the American 70,000-ton dreadnoughts. What an amazing fury that would have whipped up!

Throughout the war the Yamatos did very little, spending most of their time holed up in naval bases around the Pacific. This was mainly due to the ever present danger from submarines and carrier-borne aircraft. They did, on occasions, sally forth, usually in response to USN raids on Japanese bases, but as long as they could remain intact they, like the *Tirpitz* in Norway, comprised a 'fleet in being' and a constant headache to the Allies in the Pacific who were obliged to be ever mindful of them.

Sooner or later, however, headaches have to be tackled and these ships became the prime targets for USN carrier-borne aircraft. *Musashi* met her fate at the Battle of Leyte Gulf in October 1944. The carrier-borne aircraft of the USN must have thought it was Christmas when, below them, they saw the vast structure of the great battleship. Like bees around a honey pot the planes buzzed around her until, sustaining hits from no fewer than nineteen aerial torpedoes and seventeen bombs, she succumbed to the Pacific waters and slid beneath the waves, taking nearly half of her ship's company of 2,767 sailors with her.

The chance to tackle *Yamato* herself came less than six months later. A desperate staff in the belaboured Japanese homeland had little option but, as a last resort, to deploy her to take part in the Battle of Okinawa in April 1945 as she was the only ship remaining in the IJN that was capable of taking on the capital ships of the Allied Fleet. Ill-prepared and insufficiently protected by air cover, she headed for the coast of Okinawa. To exacerbate an already precarious situation Japan was desperately short of fuel by this time and the ship would soon need refuelling but fuel was just not available. As with her sister ship *Musashi* the previous October, the carrier-borne aircraft swooped on the great ship, which by this time was a sitting duck. With no fewer than nineteen aerial torpedoes ripping her insides apart she disappeared beneath the waves, taking 2,498 of her crew with her.

With the death of this great Leviathan it was pretty much 'all up' with Japan, which was now incapable of carrying out any major operations and an Allied invasion of Japan itself was considered imminent. On 15 August 1945, within four months of the decease of the mighty *Yamato,* the Japanese forces laid down their arms.

Italy Joins the Club

At the outbreak of the First World War Italy could boast three dreadnoughts at sea with another three in the final stages of completion. At sea was the single ship *Dante Alighieri,* a 21,600-ton battleship, which, as the country's first venture into this area, had been launched in 1910. She did very little in the war, being employed mainly as a flagship, and had the unenviable record of serving throughout the entire conflict without ever having engaged an enemy. Moreover, throughout her entire life she never once fired her guns in anger!

Of the 24,500-ton Cavour Class battleships, two – *Giulio Cesare* and *Leonardo Da Vinci* – were completed in time for the outbreak of hostilities, while the third and final ship of the class, *Conti Di Cavour,* was completed in April 1915. *Leonardo Da Vinci* was sunk in 1916, *Conti Di Cavour* suffered the same fate in 1940 and the survivor of the class, *Giulio Cesare,* was handed over to Russia in 1948 as 'spoils of war'.

Dante Alighieri – Italy's first dreadnought. Throughout her whole life she never fired a shot in anger despite being a flagship during the First World War. (Author's collection)

Andrea Doria in First World War configuration. (Author's collection)

Caio Duilio in Second World War configuration. Both ships of the class emerged unscathed from the Second World War. (Author's collection)

Following the Cavour Class the two-ship 24,700-ton Andrea Doria Class, comprising *Andrea Doria* and *Caio Duilio,* were launched in 1913 and 1914, being completed in 1916 and 1915 respectively. Both these ships survived not only the First World War but emerged unscathed from the Second World War, with both succumbing to the breakers' torches in 1956.

In various Italian shipyards there was building another class of dreadnoughts, the four-ship, 34,000-ton Caracciolo Class, which had all been laid down in 1914/15. However, only one achieved the launching stage and that was *Francesco Caracciolo,* which slid into the water in 1920 but was never completed. The other three, *Christoforo Colombo, Marcantorio Colonna* and *Francesco Morosini,* remained on the stocks until all four were delivered into the hands of the breakers in 1921.

Dreadnoughts of the Minor Navies

Austria

A soon-to-be protagonist in the First World War was Austria, which was to throw in her lot with Germany. Anxious to be counted among the more powerful of the world's navies, Austria set out to possess her own mighty battleships. Her first tentative steps into the heady realms of dreadnought building was the four-ship, 21,595-ton Tegetthoff Class, comprising *Viribus Unitas*, *Tegetthoff*, *Prinz Eugen* and *Svent Istvan*. Their launch was somewhat staggered over the following four years, probably due to financial restrictions, so that the first to career down the slipway was *Viribus Unitas* in December 1912 followed by *Tegetthoff* in July 1913. Next in line was *Prinz Eugen*, which was launched in July 1914, but the final ship, *Szent Istvan*, wasn't launched until December 1915, when the war was well under way.

Argentina

While the tensions in Europe ground inexorably onwards to the First World War, South American countries were having their own problems. This resulted in Argentina joining the dreadnought 'brigade' by seeking bids for the building of two dreadnoughts, and for two years shipbuilders from five countries vied for the contract. After a great deal of negotiating, the contract finally went to American yards, but the somewhat unconventional method employed by the Argentinians to finalise the design of these ships created a furore among the world's shipbuilders. In 1908 one of Argentina's senior officers set up in London and invited tenders from builders for the construction of two dreadnoughts and a possible third.

The guidelines nominated for the design were very fuzzy indeed, but no fewer than fifteen companies tendered designs and the crafty Argentinians perused them carefully, picking out the best bits of each, amalgamating them into one and resubmitting another call for tenders using this very revised design. They even did this a second time and finally awarded the contract for *Rivadavia* to the Fore River Company of Quincy, Massachusetts, and the contract for the *Moreno* to the New York Corporation.

Argentinian battleship *Moreno*, *c.* 1911. She and her sister ship created quite a stir in the design and tendering stages. She served for over forty years but never fired her twelve 12-inch guns in anger. (Museo Naval de la Nación, Argentina)

The shipbuilders who had taken part in the tendering were outraged, being of the opinion that their 'trade secrets' had been looted. The Argentinians, of course, were laughing, having saved close to a quarter of a million pounds on each vessel.

The result of these shenanigans was that the two ships of the 30,600-ton Rivadavia Class, *Rivadavia* and *Moreno*, named after Argentinian historical figures, were laid down in 1910 and launched in 1911. Based principally in Puerto Belgrano, they led long and very sheltered lives, being employed mainly as training ships until they kept appointments with breakers' yards in 1956.

Brazil

When Brazil decided to obtain a couple of dreadnoughts, her action sparked off an arms race in South America – perhaps not quite up to the standard of the one raging in Europe, but an arms race nonetheless – between Argentina, Brazil and Chile. Brazil led the way when, in 1907, their two-ship, 21,300-ton Minas Geraes (or Gerais) Class was laid down.

Minas Geraes – A bit of artistic propaganda at the height of the South American arms race. (Marinha do Brasil)

Minas Gerais was launched in 1908 and survived for forty-five years before being broken up in 1953. Her sister ship *Sao Paulo*, launched in 1909, lasted for forty-two years before being welcomed by the breakers.

Both vessels had been built in English yards as Brazilian shipbuilding at that time had not progressed sufficiently to cope with the required technology and skills. The lead ship had been constructed at Elswick-on-Tyne by Armstrong and *Sao Paulo* was the product of the Barrow-in-Furness yard of Messrs Vickers.

They both led quite chequered careers, being despatched to Scapa Flow during the First World War to join the Grand Fleet when Brazil entered the war on the side of the Allies in 1917. However, they were in such poor condition, not having been modernised in any way, that they were not a great asset to the Grand Fleet, so in June the following year *Sao Paulo* was despatched to the New York Navy Yard to be refitted

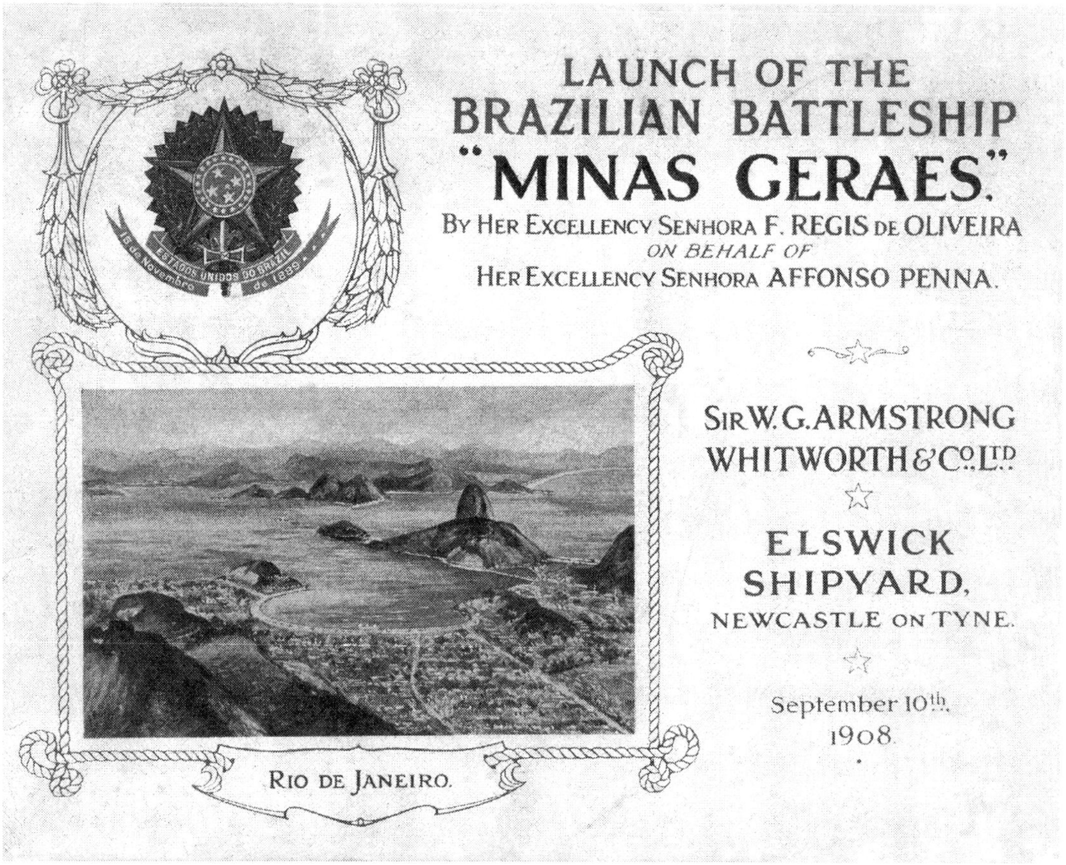

A commemorative plaque of *Minas Geraes*'s launch at Newcastle-on-Tyne. (Marinha do Brasil)

and modernised. Such was her condition that on passage she broke down and required the assistance of the USN to reach her destination. She remained in the USA for over two years and when she finally returned home her sister ship sailed to take her place in the USA to refit and modernise.

Not content with just two dreadnoughts, plans for another went into overdrive in 1911 with the 31,600-ton *Rio De Janeiro,* which was laid down in Armstrong's yard at Elswick-on-Tyne. However, by the time she had been launched in 1913 and was fitting out in Armstrong's yard, Brazil realised that with the boom in the rubber market collapsing it could no longer afford the luxury of a third dreadnought and, accordingly, she was put up for sale. The immediate buyer was Turkey who took her over in 1913, had her renamed *Sultan Osman* I and gave authority for her to continue fitting out.

She was, however, about to enter another unforeseen phase of her career. Having completed her fitting out she went to Devonport for trials, but by this time the First World War had been declared and it was obvious to the UK government that Turkey was about to throw in her lot with Germany. To prevent this powerful vessel falling

Sao Paulo. A product of Vicker's Yard at Barrow-in-Furness, she served her country well for forty-two years. (Marinha do Brasil)

into the hands of an enemy, the First Lord of the British Admiralty, Winston Churchill, ordered her seizure. Thus she passed into the control of the Royal Navy and was renamed *Agincourt*, a name that particularly took the fancy of Churchill.

With her extraordinary armament – fourteen 12-inch and twenty 6-inch guns – she was the most heavily armed battleship ever to be operated by the Royal Navy. Post-war there was a half-hearted attempt to sell her back to Brazil, but there was lukewarm response to the proposal so at the end of 1922 she wended her way to the yard of the Rosyth Shipbreaking Co.

A further battleship, the *Riachuelo*, was also planned, with the Brazilian government going so far as to place an order with the Armstrong yard at Elswick-on-Tyne, but the project fell through before she could be laid down.

Chile

In the burgeoning arms race in South America prior to the First World War, Chile was not going to be left out and accordingly her government placed the order with Armstrong's for the building of the two 32,300-ton ships of the Almirante Latorre Class. The lead ship, *Almirante Latorre,* was laid down on the Tyne in 1911, but her passage was not smooth. Launched in 1913, she had got to the stage of fitting out by Armstrong when the First World War broke out and the British government considered they had greater need of her than Chile so purchased her for the Royal Navy. She was commissioned into the Royal Navy in September 1915 and, renamed HMS *Canada,* played an active part in the First World War by taking her place in the battle fleet at the Battle of Jutland in 1916. Post-war Chile repurchased her in 1920 and, reverting to her original name, she faithfully served her government for thirty-nine years before finally being broken up in Japan in 1959.

Almirante Latorre is seen back in the Chilean Navy after her service in the British Navy as HMS *Canada.* (Museo Maritimo Nacional, Chile)

Almirante Latorre seen docked down *c.* 1930. For scale, note the diminutive figures under her forefoot. (Musco Maritimo Nacional, Chile)

Her sister ship *Almirante Cochrane*, also built by Armstrong, was also purchased by the British government, but while still on the stocks she underwent a complete redesign and emerged from the shipyard as the Royal Navy's 22,790-ton aircraft carrier *Eagle*. Needless to say she did not go back to her original owners after the war but continued to serve the Royal Navy into the Second World War, until she succumbed to torpedoes from the German submarine *U.73* in the Mediterranean on 11 August 1942.

Greece

The Hellenic government's tentative steps into the dreadnought world came to nothing. In 1912, in an attempt to keep up with their arch-enemy, the Ottoman Empire, Greece considered that she needed to modernise her navy and placed an order with a German yard, AG Vulcan of Hamburg, for a dreadnought. Their choice of builder was a great mistake, as they were to discover. The Greeks never quite made up their minds as to what the vessel should be, a battleship or a battlecruiser, but the 21,500-ton vessel was laid down in the German yard in 1913. Despite several changes in her design caused by Greece's requirement to keep up with the Ottomans, the hull was launched in November 1914. However, she couldn't be armed because the guns had been ordered from Bethlehem Steel in the United States and by this time the Royal Navy had put in place a close blockade of German ports, so nothing was able to get in. From thereon it was downhill all the way. Bethlehem sold the guns to the UK instead and they went to arm a new class of monitors, while in Germany the unfinished hull was employed as a floating barracks at Kiel. After the war it remained as a hulk in Kiel until, still incomplete, it was taken away to the breakers' yard in 1932. Just who paid AG Vulcan for their work and materials is uncertain.

The Netherlands

The Netherlands was another country that thought it would chance its arm in the dreadnought stakes, but it was just as unsuccessful as the Greeks. In 1914, with the First World War hovering just over the horizon, the Netherlands government decided to build a class of 26,851-ton battleships, which were to be laid down in 1914 and completed by 1918. The Germans, of course, had other ideas and the projected ships came to nought. Their luck didn't change in 1939 when they decided to build a three-ship class of 27,950-ton battlecruisers with the intention of reinforcing their East Indies Squadron. Once again Germany put a spoke in their wheel, with the war putting paid to their plans.

Russia: The Imperial Russian Navy

The Imperial Russian Navy (IRN) entered into the dreadnought stakes in June 1909 when the four ships of the 25,850-ton Gangut Class were laid down in two Russian yards. Two years later they had all been launched and were finally commissioned in 1914. This class, which was also known as the Sevastopol Class, comprised *Gangut,* which was finally broken up in 1958/59, *Petropavlovsk,* which became a Constructional Total Loss (CTL) in 1941, *Poltava,* which was stricken in 1925 and *Sevastopol*, which was broken up in 1957.

A three-ship class followed the Ganguts in the form of the impressively named Imperatritsa Mariya Class. Laid down in 1911 and launched in 1913/14, the 24,960-ton class comprised *Imperatritsa Mariya,* which was lost in 1916, *Volya,* which was broken up in 1936 and *Imperatritsa Ekaterina Velikaya,* which was sunk in 1918. With only five letters in her name the *Volya* must have felt quite overwhelmed in the presence of her sister ships! She had started life as *Imperator Aleksandr III,* being renamed before completion, and joined the Black Sea Fleet. She was surrendered to the Germans in 1918 but they were obliged to turn her over to the British under the terms of the Armistice. The British presented her to the White Russians. She finally ended up in French hands and was broken up in 1936

In 1915 Russia laid down another dreadnought, the 27,300-ton *Imperator Nikolai.* She was launched in 1916 but there her story came to an abrupt halt; incomplete, she was ignominiously towed to the breakers' yard in 1923.

The tentative venture into the field of battlecruisers by the Russians came in 1913 when the four 38,000-ton ships of the Borodino Class were laid down. By 1915 three of the class, *Borodino*, *Izmail* and *Kinburn,* had been launched and in the following year the last of the class, *Navarin,* roared down the slipway. However, that was the end of their careers as work on them was abandoned. Between 1923 and 1931, their uncompleted hulls were towed to the breakers.

Spain

The Spanish were somewhat more successful than the Greeks and the Dutch in that they actually built the three-ship, 15,700-ton Espana Class of battleships. *Espana, Alfonso XIII* and *Jamie I* were all built in Spain's Ferrol Dockyard and were launched in 1912, 1913 and 1914 respectively.

The lead ship, *Espana,* was wrecked in 1923, but her two sister ships each took part in the Spanish Civil War, although neither survived 1937, with *Alfonso XIII* being mined and *Jaime I* lost in the same year. In 1914 there had been a move to build another three-ship, 26,000-ton class. Though they were unnamed, one vessel became known as *Reina Victoria Eugenia,* but the other two were simply referred to as B and C. As in the case of Greece and the Netherlands, the First World War put paid to Spanish plans.

Alfonso XIII is seen on the stocks in the Ferrol Dockyard, *c.* 1910. (Naval Museum, Madrid)

Above left: *Alfonso XIII*. (Naval Museum, Madrid)

Above right: *Espana*. (Naval Museum, Madrid)

Turkey

The Ottoman Empire was also very unlucky in its sortie into the world of dreadnoughts. Having neither the knowledge nor capacity to build their own battleships, they were obliged to place their orders abroad, and chose the Armstrong Company at Elswick-on-Tyne in England. The three-ship, 24,700-ton class was to be known as the Reshadieh Class, two of which – *Reshadieh* and *Reshad-I-Hamiss* – were laid down in 1911. However, there was a delay before the last of the class, *Fatih*, was laid down in 1914, but it didn't matter a great deal as the Fates were lining up against Turkey. As seen above, the First World War put paid to a number of countries' aspirations and Turkey was no different. *Reshadieh* had rolled down the slipway in

Jaime I. At 15,700 tons, this was the smallest dreadnought ever built. (Naval Museum, Madrid)

September 1913 and by the following year was nearing completion, but with the war looming large in Europe, and in the sure and certain knowledge that the Ottoman Empire would throw in its lot with Germany, the British government was absolutely not going to hand over a brand-new battleship to a potential enemy. Accordingly, orders were issued to seize the *Reshadieh* and, renamed *Erin*, she was taken into the Royal Navy. As such she served throughout the First World War and took part in the Battle of Jutland in 1916. After the war she fell victim to the Washington Naval Treaty and was discarded in the 1920s.

Reshadieh's sister ships fared even less well. The Ottomans cancelled *Reshad-I-Hamiss* in 1912 but *Fatih,* having been launched, remained a hulk. Very little work had been carried out on her and within a few months of launch she was dismantled.

Turkey's attempt to obtain another dreadnought also fell into disarray when the *Rio De Janeiro* was purchased from Brazil. She, too, was being built in Britain and suffered the same fate as *Rashadieh,* being seized by the British Admiralty and taken into the Royal Navy as HMS *Agincourt.* In this capacity she had the privilege of being the most heavily armed battleship, British or otherwise, mounting no fewer than fourteen 12-inch guns in seven twin turrets.

Post-Second World War

If there was one particular incident in the worldwide conflict of the Second World War that surely indicated that the writing was upon the wall for the dreadnoughts, it was surely the fate of the Royal Navy's two capital ships that had been deployed to the Far East. By the autumn of 1941 it had become obvious to the War Cabinet in London that Japan was about to throw in her lot with Germany, and in an attempt to discourage this union it was decided to make a show of strength in eastern waters. One of the Royal Navy's newest battleships, *Prince of Wales* of the King George V Class, was chosen for the task and despatched to Singapore accompanied by the battlecruiser *Repulse*. It had originally been planned that the two dreadnoughts would have an escort of destroyers and an aircraft carrier. Unfortunately the carrier detailed for the job suffered a breakdown while working up off the east coast of the United States, which totally precluded her from undertaking the mission. Under the command of Admiral Sir Tom Phillips, the task force sailed from Singapore with an escort of just four destroyers. Without any air cover whatsoever the ships were in a vulnerable position and, in acknowledgement of the law that says 'if anything can go wrong, then sooner or later it will go wrong,' the Fates played a monstrous trick on the little squadron. In a position some 60 miles to the east/north-east of Kuantan, Malaya, in the South China Sea, the first wave of Japanese high-level bombers struck. The battlecruiser received a not too serious hit, but forty minutes later a flight of nine torpedo-carrying aircraft attacked. *Prince of Wales* received two serious hits, after which the ship could not be properly controlled.

There followed another attack by both torpedo carrying aircraft and by high-level bombers, but no hits were recoded. However, a third wave of aircraft achieved a devastating impact. *Repulse* was hit again and again until she succumbed to the battering, turned turtle and sank into the depths, leaving the escorting destroyers to rescue 796 of her crew. This left the battleship as the only target for the swarms of aircraft. The ship's AA armament was quickly overwhelmed, not that it had been very effective in the first place. During the whole battle only seven Japanese aircraft came to grief. With her speed reduced to a mere 8 knots she was an easy target and began to list heavily, until finally turning turtle and sinking. The escorting destroyers again came to the rescue, taking onboard no fewer than 1,285 survivors.

A battleship's 15-inch guns. (Evan Williams)

The death of a dreadnought. (US Naval History & Heritage Command)

The message was there for all to see: aircraft were the nemesis of the dreadnought no matter how well armed they were, especially if they had no air cover to protect them.

It was inevitable that aircraft would become more sophisticated but there was a limit to where the dreadnought could go. Even with the prospect of guided missiles looming, there would be no scope for improvement to the battleships. They had gone about as far as they could go and the only places left for them to go were the breakers' yards.

Acknowledgements

The author gratefully acknowledges the following for the photographs contained in this volume: Evan Williams Esq. of Taunton, Somerset, England; Luis Photos (Mrs Maria Mascarenhas) of Gibraltar; Marinha do Brasil; Museo Naval de la Nacion, Argentina; Museo Maritimo Nacional, Chile; Naval Museum, Madrid Naval Museum, Toulon; and US Naval History and Heritage Command. Thanks are due to Penny Glover and Alec Sutton for unstinting technical assistance. Finally, a special acknowledgement to my wife for her never-ending patience.

Bibliography

Burt R. A. and W. P. Trotter MC, *Battleships of the Grand Fleet* (London: Arms & Armour Press, 1982).

Colledge, J. J., *Ships of the Royal Navy* (Greenhill Books, 1969).

Coward, Cdr. B. R., *Battleships and Battlecruisers of the Royal Navy since 1861* (London: Ian Allen Ltd, 1986).

McIntyre, Donald, *The Thunder of the Guns* (London: Captain Frederick Muller Ltd, 1959).

Pears, Randolph, *British Battleships 1892–1957.*

Shurton, Ian (ed.), *Conway's All The World's Battleships* (Conway Maritime Press, 1987).